A Knight's Code
of Business

Other Business Books from PMP

Marketing Insights to Help Your Business Grow

Why People Buy Things They Don't Need

The Kids Market: Myths & Realities

Marketing to American Latinos, Part I

Marketing to American Latinos, Part II

The Mirrored Window: Focus Groups
from a Moderator's Point of View

The Great Tween Buying Machine

A Knight's Code of Business

How to Achieve Character and Competence in the Corporate World

~

Gene Del Vecchio

Illustrated by Roderick Fong

PARAMOUNT MARKET PUBLISHING, INC.

Paramount Market Publishing, Inc.
301 S. Geneva Street, Suite 109
Ithaca, NY 14850
www.paramountbooks.com
Telephone: 607-275-8100; 888-787-8100
Facsimile: 607-275-8101

Publisher: James Madden
Editorial Director: Doris Walsh

This publication is designed to provide accurate and authoritative information in regard to the subject matter covered. It is sold with the understanding that the publisher is not engaged in rendering legal, accounting, or other professional services. If legal advice or other expert assistance is required, the services of a competent professional should be sought.

Library of Congress Catalog Number:
Cataloging in Publication Data available
ISBN 0-9725290-0-4

This book uses quotes from *Don Quixote* by Miguel de Cervantes, translated by Walter Starkie, copyright © 1964 by Walter Starkie. Used by permission of Dutton Signet, a division of Penguin Putnam Inc.

Book design and composition: Paperwork

This book is dedicated to brave knights, and to their endless quest to demonstrate character and competence in the corporate world.

Contents

Acknowledgements

I would first like to thank Paramount Market Publishing for its support. The president and editor Doris Walsh and publisher James Madden immediately saw the value in this book's theme, even before the rash of corporate misdeeds hit the news. Thank you for believing in the need for a book on character and competence in business.

I want to thank nearly two dozen people who provided their thoughts, direction, or actual stories for this effort. They include Freddy Bee, Cherie Crane, Gary Elliott, Claudio Garcia, Liz Gill, Ken Goldstein, Allan Hauptfeld, Jim Hayden, Paul Kurnit, Michael Lay, Jerry McGee, Mark Rice, Ron Reilly, David Schneider, Craig Spitzer, and Sandy Wax. There were many others who provided stories and insights, but preferred to remain anonymous so that they could tell the truth without fear of retaliation. I will honor that request. It took a special person to be willing to donate misadventures. I know this because many chose not to, for various reasons. While we all have that desire to keep misadventures to ourselves, the people who contributed saw a greater good, and that was to tell a tale or two in hopes that others would learn from the misadventures they had witnessed. I thank you for your courage. To a great degree, I have eliminated company names, and the names of individuals, to keep confidences.

A special thank you goes to Gary Elliott, a long time associate and friend, who not only provided stories but also took the time to review the draft manuscript. His input was invaluable. If ever there were a true flesh and blood knight in the corporate world, filled with both character and competence, it is Gary.

I want to thank Roderick Fong, the illustrator of this book, who brought his wit and wisdom to every chapter. In particular, thank you for listening patiently to my suggestions and then always doing something better.

I want to thank Art Shulman of Shulman Research, who coordinated the survey I commissioned among 100 marketers across the United States. The insights gained helped to estimate the scope of the misadventures that exist today.

I want to thank Dutton Signet, a division of Penguin Putnam Inc. for granting permission to use various quotes from *Don Quixote* by Miguel de Cervantes, translated by Walter Starkie, copyright © 1964 by Walter Starkie.

I want to thank my wife Linda for her endless encouragement throughout my writing of yet another book. And I want to thank my children Matt and Megan for tiptoeing about the house while I was engaged in writing sentences that formed this effort.

Thank you one and all.

Foreword

My original intent was to write a book about silly misadventures in business, the kinds of events that make us laugh at ourselves. However, that is not what happened. After I completed the first draft and reviewed the "silly" misadventures, I realized that they had dramatic implications that shed light upon achieving high moral character and competence in the workplace. The stories did not make me laugh as much as they made me think.

I had lost my original intent. My stories about character and competence, I thought, would probably find no audience in today's cynical world. The whole idea of trying to achieve these virtues seemed corny, even to me, and my book seemed out of touch. Yet, I could not stop writing as the stories came too easily, and the insights grew. I tried to find humor in them, to bring the book back to my original intent, but it did not always work. The stories would not always allow it, as they began to write themselves.

Then somewhere during my second draft, the corporate world suddenly reeled with news about colossal business failures such as Enron and WorldCom. Everywhere I looked, the failures stemmed from a lack of character or competence or both. "Maybe," I thought, there is a place for a book that speaks of ideals in a world thick with cynicism. That hope kept me writing long into the night to provide what insights I could, based upon my experiences and those of many others.

My book, having started with one destination, ended at another. I believe it is better for it, and I hope you agree. Thank you for taking the time to read it.

If you have a great, firsthand story about a lack of character or competence in the workplace, write it up in a brief paragraph, eliminating the company's and people's names, and send it to me at codeofbusiness@aol.com. While I can't pay you for it, if I write another book, I might include it. I would list the author as anonymous to protect you. Thanks.

GENE DEL VECCHIO

Introduction

Overview

*"Works of invention are only good insofar as they touch the truth
or the semblance thereof, and true stories are better the more
authentic they are."*

—Don Quixote

This business book is probably not like most others you have read.
Many of today's business books have become too narrow in their focus.
Some discuss only strategy, others discuss only leadership, and still others discuss ethics—barely. They are too specialized, an unfortunate side
affect of a world that has become too complex on almost every level.
Few if any of today's business books discuss the vast array of issues, in
a simplified form, that beset today's executives.

And yet that broad discussion is precisely what is needed today, particularly as it relates to two critical fundamentals that form the basis of
all issues that modern business executives must face: moral character
and increasing competence. These are the foundations from which all
success springs, and from which every single other aspect of behavior
arises. They are the foundations on which to build a successful career
in whatever you pursue, business or otherwise. However, few books
attempt to address them both.

CHARACTER & COMPETENCE

This all seems so easy, so simple, and so obvious. All you need is increasing competence and high moral character. Yet it is not so easy or simple, and definitely not so obvious. Why? Because we make it harder than
it should be. Too many business executives today, for example, strive

for competence and neglect moral character. They care too much about self-interests alone, and ignore company interests, interests of fellow employees, and even the law. The news is filled with such sorry antics, and prisons are becoming more crowded all the time with greedy white-collar criminals. Other executives strive for character, and neglect competence. It takes effort to achieve competence, and even more effort to stay competent in a world where last year's abilities are continuously challenged by this year's issues, technologies, and competitors. Business failures caused by incompetence are legendary. Some executives, unfortunately, strive for neither increasing competence nor moral character in the executive suite. Intense self-interests make them greedy, and laziness makes them increasingly stupid. If they destroyed only themselves, it would be of little concern to any of us, but their antics have cost thousands their jobs when companies that are placed in their care collapse. Witness the recent collapse of Enron, WorldCom and others. If the accusations prove to be true, the executives who steered these modern day Titanics right into an iceberg might prove to be among the most amazingly inept and unethical people in business. We shall see.

The lessons of such high-profile corporate debacles, however, may appear to be one of ethics alone. In the press, much has been made about the allegedly low moral character of those involved, and as such, many books are apt to be written about ethics. Even business schools are rushing to launch new courses that examine ethical accounting issues. But these efforts will be too narrow, reducing the ills to one of "accounting ethics for CEOs" while ignoring a broader ethical and competence scope, as well as addressing the needs of those outside the CEO suites.

THE CHALLENGE

This book attempts to accomplish much. It attempts to address the key aspects of character and competence, and yet in an abbreviated form. Why abbreviated? The intent is to write a usable, easy-to-read *manual* that can be referred to again and again. Additionally, it would be quite easy for a book on character and competence to be lethally boring and overly preachy. So instead, I keep this manual fun and alive using illustrations, for example, that add an important but lighthearted feel to the text. I am also aware that executives have little time to read as much as they would like, so a condensed manual helps accommodate the lack of available time.

So this is a primer with an important challenge, to build the desire for increasing competence and moral character in a scant few pages.

FAILURE TALES

This book is different in other ways as well. It is not so much about success as it is about failure. It is filled with true misadventures I call *Failure Tales*. The hope is that, by telling a variety of stories of plans and actions gone terribly wrong, we might glean some learning on how we can attain great success. More importantly, this book does not take the surface approach of some other business books by stating that a leader could not lead, or that a company wasn't innovative enough. Instead, this book is about the root cause of misadventures: not about a leader who could not lead, per se, but about how a leader undermined his leadership because of an affair with an underling; not about how a company wasn't innovative enough, per se, but about how a company routinely punished failure, making employees fearful to try something new. That said, this book is a primer into the key misadventures that besiege us all, touching upon a range of maladies that serve to prevent our companies and ourselves from achieving the very best. It is about the soft underbelly of business today, that place that we know exists, but we would rather not acknowledge. It is about people, and the bad decisions they make, not just the big decisions that make the news, but about the small ones we make everyday. So while this book does address high profile misadventures such as Enron, it also delves into little known misadventures that we all face. In so doing, it is about us and about our occasional failures that account for our failures in the business world.

THE SOURCES

The knowledge and the stories poured into this book come from several sources. First, learning comes from my own 20 plus years in business. After obtaining an MBA in 1980, I ventured off to General Mills where, as an infant, I cut my teeth in the business world. Soon afterwards, I left for Ogilvy & Mather, one of the world's most venerable advertising agencies. I stayed 17 years, becoming a senior vice president (later named senior partner), responsible for Planning and Research. I also held a seat on the executive committee of the Los Angeles office. I shared responsibility for profits and losses, hiring and firing, and at various times was asked to lead training, human resources, and even company morale. The benefits of my days at Ogilvy were immeasurable. In the roles I played, both in pitching new business and stewardship of existing business, as head of research and planning as well as helping to lead the office at large, I wound up in the boardrooms of some of the most prominent corporations in America. After leaving Ogilvy and beginning my own consulting business nearly five years ago, I had the added, unique opportunity to live on the outside of corporate life, while looking in. All of those experiences combined (client side, agency side, employee, management, consultant, researcher) helped to provide insights contained within this book.

In addition, this book contains the experiences and stories of roughly two dozen mid-level and senior executives across many industries and high-profile corporations. While I was able to reference some individuals by name, others asked to remain anonymous so that they would have the freedom to tell the real story without fear of retaliation. I honored that. As I began to collect their stories and experiences, I became amazed at the scope and depth of easily avoided catastrophes that plague business today, all stemming from the same root causes: lack of character and competence. Their insights were invaluable.

Not wanting to rest the findings upon only my experiences and those of two dozen others, I commissioned a quantitative survey among a sample of 100 mid-level marketers from companies across the United States so as to reveal the magnitude of each misadventure. Throughout the book, I refer to this as *Survey of 100*. I selected *mid-level* executives (i.e. managers and directors) from the *marketing* discipline for very specific reasons. First, their mid-level status gives them a unique vantage point within their organizations. They are close enough to the top to see the actions and suspect the motives of those who control their company's destiny. They are also close enough to the bottom to see all those who may benefit or suffer as a result. I selected *marketing* executives because their role spans their organization from side to side, allowing them to come in contact with more departments than any other group, from product development and sales to research and finance. They are the eyes and ears. Because marketing in many organizations is a *line* position, those involved have the potential to make it to the very top. The marketing managers of today will be in the senior executive suite tomorrow, so their opinions and perceptions matter. Thus, mid-level marketing executives are at the right place, at the right time, in the right discipline, to provide keen insights into the character and competence of their organizations. The sample was randomly selected from a listing supplied from Dun & Bradstreet of marketers who work in companies of at least 100 people. The survey was executed by Shulman Research in August 2002 using a questionnaire administered over the telephone.

And finally, this book also dips into contemporary headlines and great books that tell the tales of great and terrible deeds, with an emphasis on the latter.

A GENTLE GUIDE

After developing the first draft, I realized that the book could benefit from a person, either real or imagined, that could serve as a model for various virtues. Contemporary, real-life examples are hard to come by, particularly in today's world. It forced me to go back into time, ages ago, to identify someone from whom we could learn. He or she did not have to be perfect, but had to be someone whose actions and beliefs would make us think. And then I suddenly discovered him. In fact, he was sitting on my bookshelf.

He is Don Quixote. This classic character, introduced in 1605 by the brilliant writer Cervantes, can teach us much about life, about living, and for our purposes, about the virtues that can make our businesses and ourselves great. His high ideals were truly inspiring, and are quoted in this book. But Don Quixote is also an unfortunate figure, for while in moments of inspired lucidity he espouses virtues that can make him great, he more often follows his delusions into one great incompetent misadventure after another. So too do we as professionals get in the way of ourselves, knowing what is best, yet following motives and delusions that become our own downfall, and the downfall of our businesses. This book holds the high ideals of Don Quixote dear. As fictional as he is, this figure has experience we can learn from.

A CALL FOR KNIGHTHOOD

The insights gained from the misadventures cited within this book, contrasted by the best we should be able to achieve, led me to one inescapable conclusion. *Today more than ever, the corporate world needs loyal Knights, brave men and women who are willing to stand up against the ills and evils that serve to infiltrate their companies and make them weaker.* The corporate world needs loyal Knights who are equipped not with armor, swords, and steeds like those who rode across Europe in medieval times, but ones of today, armed with intelligence and self-lessness to do battle with those who put their intense self interests above company interests, who value charisma more than competence. The corporate world needs loyal Knights who follow *A Knight's Code of Business* described within these pages, a code of competent and ethical behavior, intent upon righting the misadventures that befall kingdoms, so as to put them on the road to prosperity.

In a large sense, this book is *not* for CEOs and presidents. At this point in their careers, their behaviors are probably fixed, and they already have character and competence or they do not. Though I do provide guidance for them as well, *this book is really for lower and mid-level managers and executives, so that they can use it as a guide as they ascend the corporate ranks.* They are the future. This manual is to help a new generation of would-be Knights and Squires-In-Training become moral and competent Monarchs.

It is also a call for young executives everywhere to join the knight-hood. Read the book. Treat it as your manual. Think about the lessons, the stories, and the consequences of poor character and decreasing competence. Then practice *A Knight's Code of Business*. Refer to it often. Share it with all those within your realm. Inspire them to pay heed, and your company and you will avoid misadventures and benefit greatly. It is all up to you. So we begin . . .

> *"But I must tell you that there is no such thing as Fortune in the world. Nothing that happens here below, whether of good or evil, comes by chance, but by the special disposition of Providence, and that is why we have the proverb: 'Every man is the maker of his own fortune.'"*

—DON QUIXOTE

Chapter 1

Misadventures and the Kingdom

"The same happens in the comedy and life of this world, where some play emperors, others popes, and in short, all the parts that can be brought into a play; but when it is over, that is to say, when life ends, death strips them all of the robes that distinguished one from the other, and all are equal in the grave."
—DON QUIXOTE

Those are brave, insightful words from Don Quixote, indeed. Each of us plays a role in life and in business. In addition, our professional roles shift over time as our competence either increases or stagnates, and as our moral character sways to and fro, challenged and tested day to day. Though we are all equal in the grave, it is clear that most of us act as though life on this earth is eternal, and so we cherish the robes we seek as though they will be adorned forever. We constantly seek finer robes, bigger titles, more responsibility, more money, more fame, more respect. Moreover, in our own personal quest, we begin to define those around us and ourselves. Some are fortunate (or misfortunate) enough to make it to the top in their companies, while others are unfortunate (or fortunate) enough to exist at the bottom. The rest of us wallow in between, often seeking a higher role, yet sometimes falling back due to our inability to reach a higher order of competence or character.

THE BUSINESS KINGDOM

If your business kingdom is like most, it is probably inhabited by the personas wearing many robes as found in Exhibit 1. This simple structure dissects the realm by two rather crude but pervasive dimensions. Employees are either ever increasing their competence and experience or not, or they are of a high moral character or not. It is that simple. Or so it seems.

EXHIBIT 1: **The Business Kingdom**

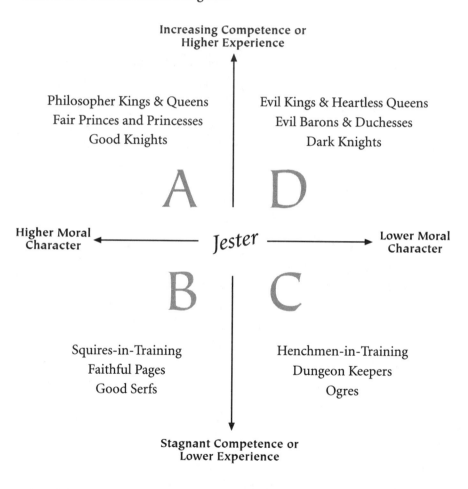

Increasing Competence or
Higher Experience

Philosopher Kings & Queens
Fair Princes and Princesses
Good Knights

Evil Kings & Heartless Queens
Evil Barons & Duchesses
Dark Knights

A   D

Higher Moral
Character ← — *Jester* — → Lower Moral
Character

B   C

Squires-in-Training
Faithful Pages
Good Serfs

Henchmen-in-Training
Dungeon Keepers
Ogres

Stagnant Competence or
Lower Experience

Competence, as will be discussed in later chapters, has many dimensions. It relates to innate talents that few can actually learn, because they are inherited at birth. These might include the gift of gab for a salesperson, or the leadership qualities of a General. Competence also includes those aspects that can be learned through study or experience, such as how to construct a balance sheet or write an effective marketing plan, or craft a piece of advertising.

Moral character has its own dimensions as well, particularly as defined in a business context. Character can often be identified by how a person balances various interests, particularly self-interests and the interests of the company. *Those who consistently place intense self-interests over company interests and other employee interests are not healthy for any organization.* They might gut the company as they seek to further personal ends. Those actions may result in greed, duplicity, and even illegality. It is the continuous focus upon intense self-interest that leads otherwise good business managers down the road of low moral character. A caveat: I am not saying that no one should ever have self-interests. We all have them, and it is healthy to do so. It's also beneficial to ensure that your interests are not overwhelmed by company interests. It is a balance. I'm really talking about individuals whose self-interests are so demanding that they make decisions that are harmful to the company as well as to their fellow employees. Interestingly, some leaders have convinced themselves that they are putting company and employee goals first, when in fact, they are subjugating the interests of the company, employees, and shareholders to achieve ends that are more personal.

Alternatively, those who more often put company interests above intense personal interests are working for the organization as a whole. Highly moral individuals also have integrity, take personal responsibility, give credit where credit is due, care about their fellow employees, and tell the truth, as painful as that may be. Low moral character means just the opposite.

Where people fall within these four quadrants, formed by the intersection of character and competence, contributes to virtually every single misadventure we see in the business world. Let me repeat: *Where people fall within these four quadrants, formed by the intersection of character and competence, contributes to virtually every single misadventure we see in the business world.*

THE ROYAL COURT AND ITS SUBJECTS

Let us examine the people more closely. Smart, extremely experienced employees who seek to gain increasing competence and routinely demonstrate high moral character, often putting their company first and their own interests second, are worth their weight in gold to any organization (Quadrant A). They include the Philosopher Kings and Queens (e.g. CEOs, CFOs etc.), the Fair Princes and Princesses (e.g. division and regional Heads, etc.), and the Good Knights (e.g. department eeads, etc.). [Note: titles may vary, and are only listed to help readers make the connection to their own organization.] These seasoned professionals have fought many battles, both in the marketplace and within their own organizations, to keep their companies on the path toward prosperity. Although some of them have reached a near pinnacle, they realize they must continually strive for greater competence, for learning is eternal. Though they are in a position of power, they do not use it for selfish ends, but continue to strive to help their company achieve its interests above their own. They know that if their company succeeds, their rewards will follow, along with rewards for fellow employees.

Seasoned professionals are charged with a great task, and they know it. They can see threats from outside and from within. They know the motives of intensely self-interested employees that can devastate a company, and they strive to prevent the many subversive tactics used by them. They run departments, divisions, regions, and entire business kingdoms, but no matter how far they rise, they keep an ear open to the employees beneath them, for they know that their competence can be greatly increased by the learning that comes from below. They are also charged with training. They must groom their successors at every level, spot those beneath them who have the high moral character and increasing competence to take their sword from them, to allow for the smooth transition of power when the time comes—and it always comes. The Good Knights (e.g. department heads) are perhaps the most important of all. First, there are so many of them and second, because they are close to both the top and the bottom. They are the glue that holds an organization together and often the first line of defense against self-interests and incompetence.

An important note: *Knighthood is not just a title, but an attitude of leadership that must permeate the entire structure, as we will discover in subsequent chapters. Knighthood is about a moment in time when the executive demonstrates high moral character, the intense desire for increasing competence, and then provides such leadership examples for others to emulate.*

Those who follow the path of knighthood also must be ever vigilant to ensure that societal interests are not put aside for the sake of company interests, for there are even larger society concerns to which a business Knight must adhere. And some Knights, so-called whistle blowers, have had momentous moments of truth, in which they found it necessary to act against companies whose evil kings demonstrated self-interests so perverse that they have harmed society at large. Such is the responsibility of knighthood. We will discuss these heroics in later chapters.

Those who demonstrate high moral character, though less blessed by either innate ability, experience, or a continual drive for greater competence are the Squires-in-Training, the Faithful Pages, and the hard working Good Serfs (Quadrant B). They may be quite competent in their roles, but they have not yet broken through to the next level of competence, either through lack of ability, experience, desire, or some combination of the above. At any time they wish, they may seek greater competence, achieve greater experience, and move upward to become Good Knights and beyond.

Executives who are smart, experienced, and desire increasing competence, yet use it to routinely put their own intense self-interests above all else, demonstrating low moral character (Quadrant D), are the Evil Kings and Heartless Queens (e.g. CEOs, etc.), the Evil Barons and Duchesses (e.g. division and regional heads, etc.), and the Dark Knights (e.g. department heads, etc.). In title and persona, they are the exact counterparts to their moral equivalents. They have an insatiable desire to feed their egos and pocketbooks first, with little or no regard for the company at large or fellow employees, unless it fits into their greater scheme and desire for control. Because they are so blessed with intelligence and experience, and they seek greater competence, they are the most dangerous foes in any organization. They are so shrewd that often they are not recognized for low moral character until the damage is done, thus unmasking their true selves. I'll save those stories for later chapters.

Those just as evil but without the innate intelligence or experience or drive for continuous competence that will allow them to make it to the highest levels of the kingdom, are the Henchmen-in-Training, the Dungeon Keepers, and the Ogres (Quadrant C). Yet, at any time they demonstrate the ability for greater competence (while hiding their true nature) they will be promoted through the ranks, stepping upon more talented people to get ahead. They are dangerous foes, particularly if they report to Dark Knights who will protect Henchmen who do their dirty work, promoting them to higher levels.

The Jesters can be found at any level, for that category is more about making people laugh than anything else. As a ratio, I believe there are as many Jesters in the executive suite as on the production line.

This rather simple classification, and the ranges within these extremes, makes up the characters you will find in any corporation, any kingdom. You know who they are. You can probably identify them easily. Importantly, they make the misadventures in business today, from larceny to duplicity.

The good news revealed by our Survey of 100 is that the business world in the United States is predominately filled with good people who try to maintain both high moral character and competence. The bad news is that the small number of consistently rotten apples can make the rest of us miserable.

Look again at Exhibit 1. Do you know which character you play and what quadrant you are in? If you want to know, jump to the appendix right now and take the Kingdom Characters Quiz by simply answering the ten questions. That will tell you what character and with which quadrant you are most closely aligned. You can even answer the questions as you think your co-workers would respond to see where they would fit. Then come back, and we'll continue our journey.

YOUR LIFE IN THE KINGDOM

Your life within this organization will be a heaven or a hell depending upon where in the kingdom you sit, to whom to report, and the nature of those who report to you. If you are a Squire-in-Training, for example, with a high moral character and desire for greater competence, your life will be blessed if you report to a Good Knight. If, however, you report to a Dark Knight or an Evil Baron, your life will be full of woe. They will gradually subvert you, cast you away, hide behind your halo, or steal your good deeds. Henchmen-in-Training who report to Evil Queens are blessed, for their low moral characters are well suited to each other. However, if a Henchman reports to a Good Knight, there is apt to be trouble. The Henchman will either be found out and cast aside, or will be smart enough to hide his true character, and more often than not, will work to poison the Good Knight and take his job. I know of many such episodes. One person I know, in particular, is a Good Knight by any measure. He works hard, and has a keen moral character. To this day, he refuses to acknowledge that he was undermined by one of his direct reports who coveted his job, and got it!

Then there are the supreme battles for control, the clashes between Fair Princesses and Evil Duchesses, between Evil Barons and Fair Princes, and every combination thereof. I have witnessed these many times, resulting in the destruction of not only the senior executives, but many of their troops as well.

The quadrants are also filled with dysfunctional people in dysfunctional roles. It is not uncommon, for example, to find an aging CEO who used to be a Philosopher King, truly gifted in character and increasing competence, who after a time stopped learning, stopped being competent in today's world. He may have the title of a King, but now has the competence of a Page. We also find loyal Pages, gifted in character and increasing competence, and capable of being department heads and more, but they have yet to be recognized by some Knight or Monarch. So they wait, become frustrated, and often leave for other kingdoms.

Find the quadrant where you now exist. Find the quadrants where those around you exist. Fill in their names on the chart. This book, among other things, will provide advice on how you can survive your particular situation.

OUR PERSONAL CHALLENGE

To make matters more fascinating, each of us is not always located in the same quadrant day to day. Because we are human beings with a complex character and shifting competencies, we might one day inadvertently play the Evil Baron when we allow intense self-interests to dominate, while the next day we may play the Fair Prince when we put company interests first. Author Malcolm Gladwell, in his book *The Tipping Point*, notes that character "isn't a stable, easily identifiable set of closely related traits . . . character is more like a bundle of habits and tendencies and interests, loosely bound together and dependent, at certain times, on circumstances and context." This means that as our daily circumstances vary, so might our character. When put into situations that entice us to exhibit low character, we very well might oblige. It can be hard to be a consistently Good Knight.

The hope of this simple approach in designating roles is this: *strive for continual competence and for consistently high moral character.* Stay in the top left Quadrant A. Know when you are shifting elsewhere, and what to do about it. Your company will be better for it, and so will you. That's the beginning of wisdom.

This book, as I said earlier, is a call to action. It is a plea for all of us to strive to attain the essence and attitude of a Good Knight, to rise up and gain control over our corporations, to right the wrongs, to avoid the misadventures, and to cast out of our kingdoms those who seek to subvert them to achieve their own ends. It is a call for knighthood, to attain the lucid wisdom and moral fiber of the best of Don Quixote, but with a competence to match.

And so each chapter concludes with a fragment of *A Knight's Code of Business*, adapted from ancient times, but made relevant for today's business climate. Each chapter also provides other advice for Good Knights, Squires-in-Training, and others to help them navigate their particular realm.

A Knight's Code of Business

Wisdom: A Good Knight strives for great wisdom, routinely promoting high moral character over low moral character, competence over incompetence, company interest over intense self-interests. Only then can all in the kingdom flourish.

And Other Advice

Good Knights, help others see the virtues that matter, help them follow in your footsteps, and beware of those who would undermine you, for they are occasionally out and about.

Good Squires-in-Training, it is your responsibility to seek guidance in character and competence. Do not wait for it to suddenly arrive. Too, if you discover that you report to an Evil Baron or Duchess, leave the court and find a Good Knight to report to, lest your life be a living hell.

Good Monarchs, wisdom begins with you and with the example you set. If you demonstrate high moral character and the desire for competence, so will your entire kingdom. Tolerance for low moral character and low competence on high breeds more of it down below, which will only seek to undermine your ability to achieve greatness, as subsequent lessons in this manual will attest.

Evil Monarchs & Barons, your desire to satisfy intense self-interests to the detriment of your company and fellow employee interests is about to be unmasked. Read on, and know that hitherto onward, you will be targeted mightily.

So we continue our journey, using stories of kingdoms far and wide that may sound strangely similar to life in your own land.

Misadventures
in Character

~

Introduction to Character

Character is defined by one's moral beliefs, and confirmed by one's actions. Attributes commonly associated with high moral character include integrity, self-discipline, sincerity, and so forth. Low moral character means just the opposite. It's pretty easy stuff, and yet not so easy.

What we define as success has shifted over the years. In the book *The 7 Habits of Highly Effective People*, author Stephen Covey points out that for the first 150 years or so of United States history, *Character Ethic* was seen as the foundation of success. This included such traits as integrity, humility, fidelity, and courage. However, after World War I, the definition of success began to shift to qualities he calls *Personality Ethic*. This was a function of such things as personality traits and public image. That shift may account for a substantial number of weaknesses we see in business today. The general public's willingness to accept personality as a component of success may have inadvertently blinded us to more enduring, significant character traits.

Still, our Survey of 100 finds our moral character is in very good shape and the number of consistent "bad apples" is few.

🛡 SURVEY OF 100

On average, our survey reported that 90 percent of employees are observed to display consistently high moral character related to their business dealings. That leaves 10 percent of employees who are not so consistent, spelling trouble for the rest of us. The range of answers was interesting, ranging from only 50 percent of employees who consistently demonstrate high moral character in some companies, to 100 percent in others.

Clearly, it matters where you work. Yet, if a company has even 10 percent of its employees whose character is in doubt, it can be devastating. We have seen that only a handful can bankrupt the largest of corporations. It is also true that those who consistently display high moral character have low character moments. In later chapters, we shall see that the incidence of lying is staggering among the general population and we don't even know that we are doing it! However, it happens, and the consequences can be dire.

While the following section speaks of high moral character, the chapter titles and content more often speak of low moral character. The reason is simple: it is easy to say that one should be honest, yet it is another thing to be able to identify and avoid situations of duplicity. That's why I have focused upon stories that more often speak to low moral character, because they help each of us to identify the subtle beginnings of such within ourselves—those damning seeds of misadventures.

We can learn something from the mysterious nature of black holes. Physicists theorize that these astronomic marvels are a never-ending implosion in which the very fabric of space-time is pulled continuously inward, so much so, that not even light can escape its clutches. One of the most amazing results of black-hole theory, reported *Discover* magazine, is that a spaceship that is caught within its early embrace will not know it. To all those on board, the ship's instruments will appear to function normally and yet, to an outside observer, the ship's own clock will begin to slow. The pilot near the black hole will not detect the change, nor will he detect that his ship is being pulled in. By the time he does, it is already too late, for once the ship enters the black hole's event horizon, darkness closes around it and the ship is ripped apart.

The point: even the best of Knights cannot always trust his or her moral compass. Things happen gradually over time, with each subtle decision and misadventure leading to the next bigger one. It is seductive and blinding. Because of this, it is always best to check in occasionally with someone you know and trust, someone who is not in the circle of decision-making where you find yourself, to check your moral compass against someone else's. That will help you ascertain if you have entered a region so filled with character black holes, that your own moral compass, while appearing to you to be in good working order, may be out of step with morality in the greater universe.

To provide some examples of low character moments, we asked our Survey of 100 to compete this sentence: "The most immoral or unethical thing I ever witnessed in my company was when . . ."

Here are some of the responses:

"A sales manager lied to a customer about the quality of a product."

"The way the sales program is administered in one part of the company. People are claiming things that don't happen, or exaggerating to make sales appear bigger."

"An employee was denied a raise he was promised."

"An employee was overpaid in the paycheck and didn't tell payroll. It took over a year to come out."

"Some personnel demonstrated less than ethical behavior in procurement—acceptance of gifts or influence. Our company fired them all."

"Upper middle managers are not candid about prospects for their products. Nobody ever wants to bring up negatives of the products."

"A manager lied blatantly, denying something he did."

"A manager used his position and asked one of his employees to make an illegal (product) purchase for him."

"A former employee made unsubstantiated allegations against a fellow employee."

"A former supervisor promised status to someone for extraordinary work and then reneged on it."

These are some of the milder examples. Cases that are more striking will be discussed in the following chapters that focus upon the key character faults resulting in aristocracy, duplicity, larceny, indecency, anxiety, maladies, and insincerity. So now, let us come to know better these misadventures of character, to guard ourselves against them.

Chapter 2

Aristocracy

"Remember, Sancho, that if you make virtue your rule in life and if you pride yourself on acting always in accordance with such a precept, you will have no cause to envy princes and lords, for blood is inherited, but virtue is acquired, and virtue in itself is worth more than noble birth."

—Don Quixote

It's a wondrous place, a palace filled with good cheer and colorful tapestries, where sweet music fills the air, where jesters tumble and tell amusing jokes for the pleasure of the nobility—those few who are in the innermost circle and have the power and the wherewithal to use it. They rejoice in what they have obtained, while yearning greedily for those precious few things that they have left to acquire.

Yes, it is wondrous within a palace where you get more than your fair share, but not always for those without, such as the serfs who toil, farming the harsh land to grow the crops or make the fabrics that the nobility uses in excess. It is a tougher life outside those gates, particularly since once or twice a week the serfs are allowed to enter the kingdom, to see the nobility and offer their goods. The workers can see what they will never touch, possibly in their lifetimes. Yet the promise is always before them that maybe, just maybe, they will some day be recognized by the king, or at least a high-ranking noble, and be allowed to live within the palace itself. So each serf works hard, for hope compels us all.

Do many American businesses operate as an aristocracy described here? Unfortunately, our Survey of 100 says "yes." Following are the percentages that agreed that their company is sometimes run as a dictatorship, an aristocracy, or a meritocracy (you'll notice that I defined each term in a very specific business context). Because companies can sometimes be run in one fashion, and at other times run as another, I allowed for double counting, which is why the percentages add to more than 100 percent.

⚔ SURVEY OF 100

Fourteen percent agreed that their company is sometimes run like a *dictatorship,* in which absolute authority is concentrated in one person who doles out rewards.

Twenty-six percent agreed that their company is sometimes run like an *aristocracy,* in which authority is concentrated in a few top executives who sometimes seem to get more rewards than their fair share.

Seventy-seven percent agreed that their company is sometimes run as a *meritocracy,* in which authority is concentrated in those truly best suited for the job, and where each person's reward is equal to his or her contributions.

Just as a meritocracy must be quite pleasant to work in, a dictatorial environment must be extremely difficult. Since the aristocracy (as I defined it for the purposes of this research) is far more prevalent today than a dictatorship, and it appears to account for so many dysfunctional companies, we will focus there. In fact, other data we will discuss shortly suggests that aristocracies at the highest levels are far more common than many employees think. Many people who are within companies that *apparently* function well do not realize until disaster strikes that their organizations are, in fact, aristocracies. Only then do the aristocratic tendencies of those involved come to light.

In his book *The O'Reilly Factor,* Bill O'Reilly makes a good case that *class* differences in America today are staggering, and "is the bottom line" for every problem he talks about in his book. I'll build upon that.

This class structure is not driven by old blue bloods, but by today's new Aristocracy found in many (not all) executive suites.

ARISTOCRACY INCORPORATED

At the top of Aristocracy Inc. are the few executives, their boards, and their divisional heads. These are the nobility, reaping the fine offerings that the remaining 95 percent of the company works hard to attain. This may sound like a harsh indictment for some companies, but there is too much proof to the contrary, particularly in the United States. Above all, at the center of an Aristocracy is a character flaw, to be described later. But first, the proof:

A report from Towers Perrin reported in *BusinessWeek* revealed that among mid-sized companies around the world, the gap in compensation between the top executives and industrial workers is the greatest in the United States. For example, in Japan the average executive compensation is 11 times the average industrial worker's pay. Contrast that with 13 times in Germany, 15 times in France, 24 times in Britain, and finally, 34 times in the United States. Said plainly, the compensation of the average executive at a mid-sized company in the U.S. is *34 times higher* than the average worker in his shop. Are U.S. executives smarter than their counterparts around the world relative to their employees, or have they simply been more astute at creating corporate environments that favor those few at the top?

Newsweek reported that "if everyone's compensation had risen as fast as a CEO's during the 1990s, the average production worker would now earn nearly $120,500" citing work done by the Institute for Policy Studies. Did some of our CEOs get suddenly smarter, faster, than the rest of us, accounting for such a dramatic rise in their income? Or did they use boards packed with cronies to get sweet compensation deals, and then use their new rock-star status to gain a new job with even greater perks somewhere else?

A study by Booz Allen Hamilton, reported in *The Wall Street Journal*, found that 34 percent of the time, the reason for ousting a CEO in Europe is poor performance, whereas in North America, 22 percent of the time the reason for ouster is related to poor performance. Are CEOs in North America truly poor performers less often, or are they smarter at dodging the bullet by using their boards of directors to save them?

The National Center for Employee Ownership discovered that 75 percent of all stock options awarded in 2000 went to the top five company executives. The next 50 executives got 15 percent of those options. The rest of the employees got 10 percent of all options. Are the rest of the employees less deserving to own a piece of the company, or has company ownership been focused upon a few who are thought to be more *entitled?* This is particularly interesting since new CEOs often get a ton of options for having worked no time at all in a company, whereas the guy on the assembly line who has worked 20 years for the same company may have no ownership whatsoever.

THE MISADVENTURES OF ARISTOCRACIES

Lucent Technologies Inc. paid $16.2 million in retention bonuses to senior executives in the beginning of 2002 reported *The Wall Street Journal.* Yet salaries had been frozen for the masses since December 2000, and roughly 50,000 people were laid off during the two years prior to the bonuses. The CEO of E-Trade collected $77 million in total compensation in 2001. Pretty good pay given that, at the time, E-Trade had since 1997 accumulated losses of $253 million, according to the *Los Angeles Times.* Because of the flap created over this apparent dichotomy, the CEO of E-Trade gave back $21 million of it. Still, that remains great compensation at a time when the company was accumulating heavy losses for shareholders.

The May 14, 2002 issue of *The Wall Street Journal* reported, "Last year may have been lackluster for bank stocks, but you would never know it from how the industry's chief executives were paid. The median CEO compensation for the 100 largest publicly traded banks rose 22 percent." I bet it helps if your buddies are on the board.

Charles Prestwood lost his retirement, about $1.3 million he had saved for over 33 years. He was not alone, for thousands of others met a similar fate. They worked for Enron. He told *People* magazine that he once believed "we had the greatest executives in the world." He could not see the aristocracy that existed at the top. In fact, that aristocracy appears to have been a very shrewd group of aristocrats, so intent upon their self-interests and personal gains that they brought down one of the largest corporations in America. Apparently, they were incompetent as well. It may happen that this becomes one of the most overt cases of aristocracy and evil princes run amuck. Yet one of the most telling comments in the Enron fiasco didn't come from an executive, but from Linda Lay, the wife of Enron CEO Kenneth Lay. She told NBC's *Today*, "Everything we had was mostly in Enron stock." She went on to claim, "We are struggling for liquidity." It was later discovered that she was not accounting for about $25 million in real estate holdings and another $8 million in other companies' stock. I guess for the Lays that constitutes a liquidity problem.

Grateful Versus Entitled, a Character Flaw

The worst part about some of those at the top of an Aristocracy is that they don't always realize that they are aristocrats. However, everyone else can see it instantly once the facts become known. Instead of displaying *gratefulness* for the wealth their company has afforded them, they begin to feel *entitled*.

 SURVEY OF 100

Sixteen percent agreed (completely or somewhat) with this statement: Some top executives here appear to feel entitled to more compensation and perks than they actually deserve.

That simple fact, from those in middle management who see it all, accounts for so much. This sense of *entitlement* grows, shows, and distorts common sense. Enron reportedly paid about $100 million in retention bonuses to top executives just days before it announced bankruptcy. In 2000, Enron apparently paid $140 million to Kenneth Lay when the company's entire net income was only $975 million. What of the masses at Enron? Let them eat as much cake as $13,500 will buy, for that was the cap on severance payments for all those let go.

CEOs should be compensated fairly, based upon merit and true contributions. Many CEOs are worth enormous sums, because they have made enormous sums for shareholders and have kept their firms growing and their employees thriving. The difference is this: when company profits suffer, CEOs and senior executives should suffer as much if not more than the serfs, particularly since senior executive mismanagement is often responsible for the company's downturn. When executive compensation does not suffer in accordance with the downturn, or if executives get a good chunk of the company's entire profits, you can tell that an Aristocracy is in full swing. The April 15, 2002 issue of *BusinessWeek* published a listing of companies with the lowest shareholder returns. Cisco Systems, for example, had a shareholder return of -22 percent (that's *minus* 22 percent) over the previous 3 years, yet the chief executive, John Chambers, received total pay of about $280 million over that same three-year period. Though that sum might have been predicated upon the gains in earlier years, it is clear that the compensation committee may have been overly giddy and generous during the hi-tech heydays.

At the core of this is human weakness that virtually all misadventures come down to. During times of suffering, profits, or even languishing growth, Aristocrats do not believe they should relinquish their entitlements. Instead, they let the masses pay, in one way or another.

The *LA Times* reported, "Starbucks Corp. agreed to pay as much as $18 million to settle claims that thousands of current and former managers and assistant managers in California stores were forced to spend long hours performing menial tasks and then cheated out of overtime pay." They were not alone. Farmers Insurance Exchange was told by a jury to pay $90 million in overtime pay, and Pacific Bell agreed to pay $35 million for the same.

Let's pause a moment and review the definition of the word Aristocracy. From World Book Online Americas Edition: *Aristocracy is a high social class that often used to include the government leaders of a state or nation. Its members claim to be, or are considered by others to be, superior to other people in the society because of family ties, social rank, wealth, or ability. Historically, the word aristocracy referred to a form of government controlled by a few wealthy or socially prominent citizens.*

Is there any doubt that this definition describes some companies in the world today?

I was born into a blue-collar family. Both of my parents worked the assembly line. In fact, when my father went off to fight WWII, my mother helped assemble bombs in the production line, making her, along with millions of other women of that era, the fabled Rosie the Riveter. As my brother, sister, and I grew up, I remember my mother working one job in a factory, while my father worked two. He would get home long enough to have dinner, and then bolt for the evening shift at a different assembly line in a different company. They somehow made it work. I was the first of my family to get a bachelor's degree, which was amazing to begin with, and I astonished my family further when I got an MBA. My point is this: I think my background led me to greatly appreciate what I have today. I was not born into an "entitled" family. Because more and more executives today come from white-collar, professional families, they may begin their careers with high goals, which in itself *may* sow the seeds of entitlement, thus fostering the aristocracy. I often worry that my own kids, now being raised in my white-collar family, will begin to demonstrate more entitlement than gratefulness as they seek employment.

Aristocrats Believe They Are Special Human Beings

When the "us versus them" mentality begins to take hold in aristocratic companies, it can have an impact on absolutely everything. Some senior executives come to believe they are not just special professionals, but *special as human beings as well*, and so they are entitled to be treated as special humans. This brings me to a little personal story, a little misadventure.

There I was, rocketing up an elevator to the executive floor of a major U.S. corporation, arriving a bit early to deliver a strategic presentation that would precede a review of new advertising. The first to arrive, I walked into the glass conference room and arranged my presentation materials to ensure that everything was accounted for and ready. With 15 minutes left before the CEO Monarch and entourage would arrive, I looked through the glass wall separating the executive conference room from the hall, and noticed an alcove that I suspected was a restroom. I decided to freshen up before my presentation. I tentatively opened the door. It was not identified as a restroom, yet it was as I had suspected. Moreover, it was, without a doubt, one of the nicest restrooms I had ever been in. Sparing the details, I'll simply say this: I had the same reaction upon entering the facility as Dorothy had when she first opened the front door of her home and peered into Oz, making her black and white world suddenly dazzle with color. "Wow," I thought, "Nice restroom." I was in the facilities for less than five minutes and then left, much better for the experience. I made sure it was exactly as I had left it. Works of beauty should be left as such.

As I departed, a security guard suddenly confronted me. He gazed hard into my eyes with a Clint Eastwood stare, as if he suspected I had just stolen his cattle. He asked me what I was doing. Modesty prevented me from telling the whole truth, so I said I was just freshening up in preparation for my presentation to his CEO. He informed me that I was in THE CEO's restroom, and that was not acceptable. "Ah," thought I. "This is the royal palace guard." He glanced over his shoulder at the conference room where I was to deliver my presentation, and told me I could return to it. As I reentered the conference room, I saw him through the glass wall as he radioed for help. "What on God's earth did I do now?" I thought. Here I am, ready to deliver a presentation, and I'm going to be hauled away for using someone's restroom. Then it occurred to me. He thinks I sat upon the royal throne!

A minute later, a woman appeared with a rag in one hand and a bottle of heavy duty cleaner in another as though she was on her way to clean up a toxic chemical spill in downtown Los Angeles. She rushed into the restroom, and then reemerged a minute later, a look of relief on her face. She shrugged her shoulders at the guard, an unspoken "No toxic spill here." Then she left. The guard slowly walked back down the hall, and gave me one last, long look as though to say, "Don't even think about it."

As I presented to this particular Monarch a few minutes later, I couldn't help but think that though we were a few scant feet apart, it might well have been light years. The Monarch jetted about with the

Beautiful People and I spent my spare time at Home Depot trying to find fittings for my plumbing. The Monarch was the CEO, and I a *mere* senior vice president. But serfdom is not about title. It's about how those above you make you feel, either intentionally or inadvertently. The palace guard, the toxic waste attendant, and I were serfs to the Monarch, for it was decreed. Even in those respects where we should be treated as equals, we are sometimes not.

However, there is no serfdom for those who refuse to be treated as such. As Don Quixote told Sancho, "*have no cause to envy princes and lords, for blood is inherited, but virtue is acquired, and virtue in itself is worth more than noble birth.*"

To Appease or not to Appease

Even in the best of companies, there is a special aristocratic attitude that many people have, from monarchs to serfs. Some have an innate talent for immediately assigning co-workers into two groups: those they need to appease and those they do not; those who are worthy of attention and those who are not. You see it most clearly in the simple act of returning telephone calls. While it is simply good manners to return all calls, people with an aristocratic attitude return some calls and not others, because they deem some people more worthy than they deem others. I have noted countless times that when certain co-workers are promoted, they deem themselves suddenly "special" and gradually begin the process of reducing the number of telephone calls they return. I have also noted that there are many others who are promoted, yet continue to treat each telephone call (and person) equally and return all calls. The former are trying to tell the world that they are now special, and you are not. They elevate themselves by treating you as a "commoner." Though many will claim they are now too busy (or never got your message), this is often just an excuse to hide their aristocratic tendencies. It is quite funny when you see some assistant, who was the most reliable person, suddenly shift to this attitude as he or she rises up the ladder. It connotes that, in truth, there was an aristocrat just dying to be unleashed. Beware of them. This is not just about bad manners; it is about class strata and entitlement.

There's an ugly side to some people that leads to prejudice. It's the worst form of aristocracy. Since we spend so much time in our business kingdoms, we encounter people of all races, creeds, ages, and sexual orientations, not to mention genders. The beliefs and attitudes we bring from home and our upbringing are apt to influence our working relationships. When in-bred biases negatively influence our ability to judge people fairly, solely by their contributions in the work environment, it is truly sinister. Much time and effort is spent righting wrongs done to people who simply want to be measured by their contributions. However, some humans judge unfairly, and so we end up in court.

The U.S. Equal Employment Opportunity Commission states that in 2001, a total of 80,840 charges were filed for the many types of discrimination. These include discrimination based upon race, sex, age, disability, national origin, and religion. The amount of money and resources spent is formidable. The monetary benefits awarded for some of these categories in 2001 (not including monetary awards obtained through litigation), totaled $94.4 million for sex-based charges, $86.5 million for race-based charges, and $47.9 million for disability-based charges.

THE EMPLOYEES' MAGNA CARTA

Productivity suffers when people see the rewards of their labors given disproportionately to others, and when they are treated as second-class citizens. They work less. Care less. They become less willing to offer new ideas, especially to those that will take those ideas and benefit themselves. It becomes harder for any of us to give our all when we partake so little in the fruits of our labors, and yet pay so dearly when those in management are incompetent in running the business.

Shareholders, the ones who really own the kingdom, are fighting back. The amazing thing about today's shareholders is that they are increasingly made up of rank-and-file employees who own company stock either directly, or, more frequently, through institutional investors like mutual and pension fund management companies. In time, this may have as great an impact on the corporate world as the Magna Carta did in feudal England, when it guaranteed greater rights to the English Barons in 1215, thus weakening the authority of King John. The Magna

Carta became a model, which later guaranteed greater rights to all English people.

A June 2, 2002 edition of the *LA Times* reported, "shareholder activism has been a weapon of choice recently." Resolutions at EMC Corporation and Bank of America Corporation have sought to constrict executive pay. In fact, at a Bank of America annual meeting in 2002, shareholders limited severance-pay packages for top executives. Other shareholders are demanding more directors who are independent of the company, to break up the love fest between a CEO and his cronies and family on the board. CEO beheadings are also on the rise. It seems that there are Knights on some boards in America. Aristocrats beware.

MONARCHS WHO REFUSE ENTITLEMENTS ARE THE ONES THAT GAIN

Thankfully, while many companies may have aristocratic tendencies, they are not destroyed by them. It is also the case that true Philosopher Kings and Queens *do* exist in the business world—people who understand that by giving up entitlements, they actually gain more in loyalty and influence.

One such Philosopher King is the talk show host Jay Leno. He may look and talk like a jester with a quick joke and self-deprecating persona, but he appears to be as regal and powerful as they come. NBC's *Tonight Show with Jay Leno* is the most popular late-night show on television, according to *TV Guide*. It went on to note that while Leno brings home about $17 million a year, his rival Dave Letterman brings home about $31.5 million. Leno shrugs it off with "How much money do you need?" I'm willing to bet that Leno is a man who feels grateful, not entitled. That's one of many qualities that separates Philosopher Kings and Queens from aristocratic ones. Employees love leaders who resist riches and power and work every bit as hard as they do themselves. Gratefulness breeds intense loyalty that fosters greater allegiance and productivity, which in turn, pays off for all concerned. Weeks after the *TV Guide* interview, Leno called about 200 of his staff together, and in appreciation of their hard work, gave out about $1.5 million *of his own money!* In that moment, his power and influence grew, allowing him to gain far more than he had lost. Importantly, it is not Mr. Leno's success that has led to his personal values. His values led to his success. In his book *Jack, Straight From the Gut*, former GE CEO Jack Welch explains his involvement in hiring Jay Leno [NBC is owned by GE]. The debate was whether *The Tonight Show* should select David Letterman or Jay Leno to replace Johnny Carson. Welch weighed in. "You know I'm not qualified to pick either one," he told his executives. "But if I were you, I would do this: I'd go for GE values. You like Leno's values. He's good for the affiliates. He's a good human being. The American public will find out that's true."

The Lord of the Rings comes to mind. Why did Tolkien craft a story in which he gave the most powerful of rings to a little Hobbit? Because the Hobbit could resist wielding the power for his own self interested ends. And that's what distinguished true good from true evil—the simple act of resistance. Those who resist the power given to them actually obtain more power through loyalty and friendship. Those who abuse it run the great risk of being shunned and usurped.

BE EVER VIGILANT

Sometimes events surprise you, forcing you to look hard at yourself. I was at Ogilvy & Mather in 1989 when it was purchased for $864 million by WPP, a U.K.-based company that went on a buying and investment rampage in the 1980s and 1990s. It was not the most pleasant takeover. Once it occurred, Martin Sorrell, CEO of WPP, stripped the office heads of much of their decision-making ability. I was on the executive committee of the Los Angeles office at the time. Before the takeover, we were given a profit objective and then were allowed to do much of what we needed in order to meet the objective. Hire people. Fire people. Give raises. Delay raises. Whatever. The power was mostly ours to command. After WPP took us over, increasingly our hands were tied. We were no longer given just a profit target; it was now necessary for us to explain our raises, to get them approved, to justify our headcount, and so on, all the way up the ladder to WPP headquarters in many cases. In short, we lost most of our power and our freedom to run our own offices. To be fair, Ogilvy was not in the best of shape financially, and a bit of financial handholding was probably warranted. However, to us, it felt quite exaggerated.

At a senior partners' meeting in New York a year or so later, Martin Sorrell arrived and spoke to a hundred or so of us about his vision to bring WPP and Ogilvy to heightened profitability. It was not the warmest meeting. During the Q & A, he received several heated questions. Mine was one of these. I told Mr. Sorrell that I was concerned that he had stripped each office of its decision-making ability and asked when he would return greater authority to us.

I was thunderstruck at his response. Martin Sorrell said that when he took over Ogilvy, he was surprised at the number of "Barons" that existed—landowners that were guarding "their turf" as opposed to working for the benefit of the company as a whole. He said that until he felt comfortable that all were pulling for the company, not their individual fiefdom interests, he would not relinquish the power.

In sort, he saw some of us—and me I suppose—as part of an aristocracy. It made me think hard about whether we were really interested in Ogilvy, or just in the Los Angeles office. Was Martin Sorrell a monarch, or was he a statesman who was being vilified by nobility he sought to dismantle? I'm not sure where the truth lay. However, after that day, I thought more about the greater Ogilvy and less about Los Angeles. I thought more about our people and less about me. I gave a raise meant for me to one of my employees. I refused several perks usually given to my position, like annual passes to a private gym. I could not justify taking such perks when we were routinely faced with salary freezes and layoffs. I learned a lesson, born from an observation from a distant king (who later was knighted for real, and became Sir Martin thereafter).

THE MERITOCRACY

While I was putting my own little department in order, Shelly Lazarus who became CEO of Ogilvy, shifted on a far grander scale. She vowed to transform Ogilvy into a "meritocracy," where each would be rewarded based upon their merit, and merit alone. "It's simply about judging people by what they contribute," Shelly recently told me, "and not to be influenced by where they went to school or what they look like. It's not so much a system as a way of thinking." When she took over the reins of Ogilvy, she fired some high-profile executives who were not pulling their weight, in order to send a message to the organization as a whole while at the same time freeing resources for those that contributed more. It is difficult for any company to consistently achieve a true meritocracy. However, Shelly made the effort and I noted it.

The notion of a meritocracy is simple: people should get paid in accordance with their worth in the marketplace (supply and demand) and their contributions to the company's performance. Worth in the marketplace is often assessed by looking at industry averages and high-low ranges for people with similar titles and years of experience. Many industries collect such data. Recruiters add another spin, because they provide data on what it takes to entice people to leave their jobs and join a new company. It can add as much as 20 percent to the range. That gives any employee a sense of marketplace worth. However, once a person is inside the castle walls of any given kingdom, "merit" is also determined, as noted, by accomplishments that enhance company performance. Various factors come into play, but the most basic are these: employees should know what is expected of them the day they are hired. They should know the performance criteria. They should be reviewed to ascertain if they are meeting these objectives, and they should know what their "carrot" is for having done so. The carrot could be a certain level of raise, a bonus, or whatever. Then, they should get the carrot if they complete their objectives satisfactorily.

It is good to note that 77 percent of our survey agreed that their company is *sometimes* run as a meritocracy, yet *sometimes* is not *always*.

Never once in my career or the careers of many others I know, have I witnessed a meritocracy run consistently and smoothly. Not once, though I saw many good people try. Instead, objectives are often mysterious and vague, performance reviews sporadic, and raises often have more to do with "what's available" than "what did you merit." Moreover, this happens even with bosses who do their very best to be "fair."

Meritocracies start at the very top with a concrete plan. If it doesn't exist there, it exists nowhere. It is the only way to ensure that "merit" is spread throughout the kingdom, rather than "entitlements" poured thick at the very top. In engrained aristocracies, there are so many entitlements at the top (in the form of compensation, cars, loans, stock options, bonuses, and other perks) that there is nothing left for "merit" at the bottom. That, in a nutshell, is the problem with aristocracies.

A Knight's Code of Business

Meritocracy: A Good Knight creates and defends meritocracies in the workplace, because such a system recognizes those who achieve, and compensates them accordingly.

And Other Advice

Good Knights, you must constantly refuse to be pulled into the aristocracy's embrace, for it happens bit by bit until you have lost your true self and begin to feel entitled rather than grateful. Beware of Evil Barons and others who seek grand entitlements, and unmask them, lest they starve others who merit more.

Good Squires-in-Training, demand to be paid based upon merit, and if the aristocracy will not allow it, find a meritocracy that will. Knights have already learned that lesson.

Good Monarchs, this is a new age. You cannot expect people to stay with you out of loyalty, while paying them less than they can get in another kingdom. Pay them for their contributions, and you will not only inspire them, but you will entice the best from other kingdoms. Also, be aware that the compensation you receive will be scrutinized by those within your kingdom, leading to envy and hate if your contributions are lower than your rewards. Lower productivity will follow, and your kingdom will not achieve its full potential.

Others, if you are a shareholder, you must let your voice be heard. Elect directors that matter, ones who are independent from top management, who can institute truly fair independent audit and compensation committees. Make directors and management accountable. Fire them if need be. If you are on a board of directors, do not be blinded by the rock-star status and charisma of leaders you seek to employ, for you will be paying extra for their popularity rather than for what their abilities merit. Fat compensation schemes you give them upon hiring will come to haunt you when these rock stars fail.

Chapter 3

Duplicity, Lack of Integrity

"Therefore, if you think that this devil you speak of smells of amber, either you are deceiving yourself or he is deceiving you by making you believe he is not the devil."
—DON QUIXOTE

An aristocrat believes that there is truly a difference between he or she and the masses, and those differences manifest themselves in ways that are both professional and human, fueled by a sense of entitlement that overrules gratefulness. However, that does not necessarily mean that an aristocrat lies or uses subterfuge or breaks promises. Some do, and some don't. Lies, broken promises, and subterfuge are reserved for those, aristocrats and others, who take a step toward much larger misadventures involving a lack of integrity, deception and the two-headed beast, duplicity.

Evil Barons, in particular, are especially deceptive because they are very competent in what they do. In their efforts to reward themselves at the expense of their companies and fellow employees, and using deception to achieve those rewards, they foster webs of conflict and controversy that become highly unproductive to the goals of the company itself.

🛡 SURVEY OF 100
On average, our respondents said that nearly 11 percent of the time the rank and file employees act in a deceptive fashion in the workplace in order to get ahead, and that 11 percent of the time top executives do the same.

I have experienced such incidents first hand, as have we all. The most insidious events occur when Evil Barons are disguised as Good Knights. Whereas Ogres are easy to spot because they are too stupid to conceal their efforts, Evil Barons are cunning, and many times run unnoticed, or if recognized, they often escape punishment. Such was the case with one.

THE BAD SEED

Once upon a time in a glorious realm, a company formed a team of Good Knights and Squires in order to develop the strategic direction for a brand so immense that it touched nearly every soul in America, and still does. The King of this realm decided that he wanted a third party to assist the team by providing some input based upon this person's past experiences. So this person was brought in to aid in this one assignment. He looked like a Good Knight. He walked like a Good Knight. He talked like a Good Knight. However, little by little, as time went on, his true nature was slowly revealed. He was not a Good Knight at all, but an Evil Baron.

The Evil Baron began to force his opinions upon the team about how the brand should be positioned in the marketplace. However, the Baron's point of view could be justified only by his *intuition*, not by the facts, which startled many of the experienced Good Knights on the team. And worse, the Evil Baron appeared to crave power and worked in ways to gain it. His actions pit department against department, team member against team member, and camps began to form. There were a few who agreed with his direction and recommendations, and many who did not. It split the team.

A Good Knight recognized what was happening and enlisted the help of other Good Knights and Good Squires. They used their power to rein in the Evil Baron. They did not invite him to key meetings for a short time because his very presence was disruptive. In so doing, they rebuilt relationships with other departments. And it worked. The renewed team crafted the strategy for the very important brand in a way that best fit the situation, backed by the data at hand. The Evil Baron was slowly allowed back into the team, as a sign of goodwill.

The strategic direction, crafted by the Good Knights, was presented to management. It was extremely well received by the company and instantly adopted. The brand flourished mightily under the new direction, and continues to do so to this day.

Now, the King had remained oblivious to all the events that had transpired between the Good Knight and the Evil Baron. Why? The Good Knight, not wanting to disturb the King with word of trivial battles in the courtyard, did not speak of the Baron's disruptive nature. However, unbeknown to the Good Knight, the Evil Baron had kept a strong line of communication to the King, and gave the Monarch the impression that the Baron had led the project. This belief was fostered by the Good Knight himself, who had given the Evil Baron a role in the presentation as a gesture of teamwork. The Baron performed magnificently, and in the presence of the King, took more credit than was his due. In fact, the King decided to hire the Evil Baron full time, for he was not the wiser.

What of the true Good Knight who was responsible for bringing the team together? He was banished from the kingdom. That's right, he was fired. It seems the monarch thought he was "not on the same team and counterproductive to the direction the brand had to go in." Odd, since the Good Knight was the chief architect of the entire plan. It makes you wonder just who gave the King the opposite impression.

Guess who replaced the Good Knight. That's right, the Evil Baron. But it didn't last long. He eventually left the company for a bigger job somewhere else. He then left that job for a bigger job somewhere else. And so on. One must wonder how many Good Knights were sacrificed to push forward the career of this one Evil Baron. And there are Evil Barons everywhere.

Now, appearances are a matter of perception and the Evil Baron in this story could believe that he was a Good Knight and that the others were Evil Barons. That's possible, though the others are sticking to their perceptions.

In ancient fairytales there are creatures known as changelings. These are ugly fairy babies. Fairy mothers trick human mothers into caring for these fairy babies. A fairy mother does this by stealing the healthy human baby, and replacing it with her ugly fairy baby; hence the term, *changeling*. Once in the human home, the ugly fairy baby creates havoc. Nature goes one step further. There are several types of birds such as cowbirds and cuckoos that are changelings (also known as brood parasites). They do not create their own nest, nor do they sit on their own eggs. Instead, they lay their eggs in the nests of other birds. When the eggs hatch, they dominate their stepmother's attention, and even push the mother's real hatchlings out of the nest. After the changeling baby gets what it needs to mature, it flies away to lay its own eggs in a nest of another unsuspecting mother (who often doesn't recognize the difference). When these new eggs hatch, they will dominate the stepmother's resources for selfish ends again, killing the mother's real brood, and then flying away again.

This is real stuff. There are self-interested, dangerous Barons, Kings, Queens, Duchesses, Dark Knights, Henchmen and others out there. They may be few, but they use duplicity to weave their way into organizations, appearing under a banner of righteousness, in order to achieve selfish ends. They create havoc. Their self-interest is endless, and they are often intelligent enough so that no one realizes the extent of the damage until it is too late, or not at all. They arrive in companies as saviors, begin pointing fingers, and blame everyone for the company's woes. It draws attention away from their ambitious nature. It is not uncommon to hear of a new CEO being installed, and one of his first acts is to "sweep" management clean so that he can bring in his own people. Are the people he fired truly dead weight, or is the new CEO simply purging anyone who might offer resistance? Good Philosopher Kings and Queens take great pains to understand the strengths and weaknesses of the people they inherit before they reach conclusions. Evil Monarchs move fast.

Moreover, unfortunately, Good Kings are duped, and Good Knights are often the first to be purged, for Evil Barons fear them the most. Evil Barons always operate the same. Arrive. Point fingers. Divert attention. Poison Good Knights. Plunder the royal treasury. Move on.

What is the moral of this tale? Both Good Kings and Good Knights need to be ever alert, for they can easily be blinded and undermined by those whose intentions are greatly motivated by self-interests.

Deception and lying is where it all begins, this path to low moral character and low integrity, and Evil Barons can become Evil Kings. Here is a brief story from a contributor, a very senior executive today, who prefers to remain anonymous:

Anonymous Storyteller

In the mid-1980s, I was the director of marketing for a small high-tech company. The CEO thought he was better than everyone else, and in a Gordon Gekko way, he felt that one reason he was better than others was that he did not feel obliged to follow the same moral principles that restrained others. In fact, in one heated conversation, where he was berating me for not living up to his standards, he yelled, "The difference between you and I is that you don't feel it is OK to lie and I do!" (It is actually quite difficult to counter that particular put down, when it comes from your boss.)

The particular situation that led to that conversation was an upcoming sales meeting. I was supposed to assure our sales reps that we would be producing large quantities of our new hit item. I knew this would never happen, though, as we were behind in planning and we did not have enough funding to pay for much production. Well, I found a way to hedge with the reps in a way that pleased my boss, without compromising my stake in a pleasant afterlife, and the reps went out and sold the heck out of this item, as my boss wanted. Of course, we could not deliver against the orders, and our retailers were furious with us and told us they would not support us in the future. This was clearly a case of crime (or at least lying) doesn't pay, because we went bankrupt within a year.

Low moral character may pay in the short term, but rarely in the long term.

A TALE OF INTEGRITY LOST AND PROMISES BROKEN

Once upon a time there was an Ice Castle Kingdom in a frozen wilderness that produced products that virtually every human in America has consumed, and still does. The Monarch decided he needed new advertising so two advertising agencies were selected to pitch the Monarch's business. One agency came from the Middle Lands, whereas the other hailed from the Western Lands. The agencies were told that they were to develop a strategy (positioning) and the advertising based upon that strategy. Then the work of both agencies would be put into a research test. It was a joust. The agencies were also told that the one that produced the highest-scoring advertising would be selected, provided it met the testing norms or averages. The agencies agreed, and went off to toil.

After a time, both agencies submitted their work, and both pieces of advertising were put into the research test as promised. The agencies then were called to the Ice Castle Kingdom to discover the result, and it was this: The work submitted by the agency from the West won. It bested the other agency's work considerably, and was comparable to the norms. This was due mostly to a superior positioning strategy that proved most effective. But lo, rather than award the business to the agency from the West as agreed, the marketing team from the Ice Castle Kingdom decided that the agency's work did not test "high enough," despite the fact that it met the criteria as originally set. And so the Ice Castle Kingdom decided to redo the joust, allowing each agency to try again.

A Good Knight from the agency of the West was furious, flew back to his own Monarch, and pleaded that the agency withdraw from the joust. "The Ice Castle Kingdom proved to be duplicitous," said the Good Knight, adding that the agency of the West should not waste any more resources trying to appease the Ice Castle Kingdom, or its Monarch, or its marketing staff, as it would lead to no good. The Ice Castle Kingdom lacked integrity, and that was not the beginning of a good relationship, even if the agency eventually won the business, said the Good Knight.

However, the Monarch of the agency of the West disagreed and sent his Good Knight forth to develop a second round of advertising. Again, both agencies submitted their work, and both pieces of advertising were tested. This time, while both pieces of advertising did well, the advertising from the agency from the Middle Lands was more effective, and was immediately awarded the business.

"How could this be," wondered the Good Knight from the city of the West, "for our strategy was superior to begin with?" Easy; the client had, prior to the second joust, given each agency the other's research results. That allowed the agency of the Middle Lands to learn from the other agency's initial success. The Western agency was, in effect, competing against its own strategy. The Good Knight swore upon his sword to never, ever work with clients who demonstrated such duplicity again. And so he hasn't. I suppose you could say that the client did a smart thing, by acting in somewhat deceptive ways in order to get the best work for its company. However, another client might have kept to the original bargain, awarded the agency in the West the business, and then worked with them to achieve even higher scores. You decide.

The small act of keeping promises is not what it used to be.

I was recently in Phoenix in the back of a taxi, zipping in and out of traffic on my way to conduct research for a client. The cab driver and I were discussing the weather, then the Arizona Diamondbacks baseball team, and finally I asked him how he became a cab driver. He said that he had started a couple of businesses before becoming a cab driver, but they all ended up in bankruptcy. "This is a great country," he concluded with an earnest smile as he peered over his shoulder and into my eyes, "because when you fail, they forgive your debts!" I thought about his comment a lot over the next couple of days, and then decided to add these paragraphs to this book.

While bankruptcy law has numerous benefits (like avoiding the debtor's prison of years past), it has a downside. Legality has replaced character. It is not so much about what *you should do* any more, but about what the law says you *must* do. If you satisfy the law, many people today think that somehow you have satisfied the demands of moral character. Is that true?

Let's contrast the taxicab driver's comments with the actions of someone else. This other man was born in 1835. He worked several jobs during his youth and manhood but achieved notable success as a writer. Unfortunately, he proved in later years to be a terrible businessman. He lost a fortune in an investment in an automatic typesetting machine, and around the same time, started a publishing company that failed miserably in 1894. This left him with heavy debt (promises) of over

$100,000. According to the bankruptcy law and agreements with creditors, this man was required only to pay half of what was owed. However, that was not good enough for him. *He decided to pay what he owed in full, keeping his promises in full.* He was quoted as saying that "honor is a harder master than the law." So despite bad health and an aging 60-year-old body, he went on a worldwide tour that lasted years and gave lectures to earn enough money to pay back every dollar he owed. When he returned years later, *The New York Times* said he "has shown that the American standard of honor goes beyond the standard set by the law."

The American populous figuratively knighted this man, for they saw a character ethic that transcended laws. Principle was involved, and he felt compelled to set it right. How ironic that a man so knighted wrote a wonderful story about *A Connecticut Yankee in King Arthur's Court.* This man, Mark Twain, was a Knight in every sense of the word. He kept promises. He achieved integrity. He was deemed a true American hero, as much for his integrity as for his writing.

The number of people who applied for bankruptcy in the United States hit a new record for a 12 month period—over 1.5 million from mid-2001 to mid-2002. Formal bankruptcy will save many families from further hardship. That's good, but how many in today's world will exhibit the character that Mark Twain possessed over 100 years ago? Few, if any.

FROM EVIL PRINCE TO STUPID OGRE IN ONE MEETING

All forms of duplicity and lack of integrity ooze their way about the office. There I was, working in an advertising agency, in a meeting with a wonderful team dedicated to winning a new piece of business. I was the head of planning and research. The account manager, a vice president with some stature, presided. We debated the merits of various courses we should take to win the business, and then reached consensus. It was glorious; the free exchange of ideas, the way in which the account manager solicited all opinions, the way he worked to inspire debate and then push toward a resolution that truly built upon the opinions of all. The next day, we met again as a team to present our approach to the head of our office, our Monarch. The account manager began the meeting with a reference to the meeting the day before and the wondrous ideas generated, with a pronouncement that all of the ideas he was now to present were the group's effort. It was a nice opening, patting all of us on the back before the meeting even began.

However, as the account manager began to speak and outline *our* ideas, the meeting took a decided turn. The plans he outlined were his *own*, and resembled no part of the consensus we had reached the day before. At that moment, I suspected he was an Evil Prince. As the team leader, he could have imposed his view. Good team leaders are required to gather opinions, but sometimes have to make the tough call of following their direction instead, based upon their experience and the evidence. That happens. However, this apparent Evil Prince led the group into thinking that all of our ideas were wondrous and accepted. Then, to gain the King's approval, he led the King into thinking that we had reached consensus, when we had not.

Without Truth, There Is No Trust

The office head, our King, listened to the Evil Prince's ideas, his eyes flashing at some of the more outlandish ones, but he remained quiet until the end. Then he paused. "We are all in agreement with this?" asked the King as he scanned the team members, his eyes landing hard on mine, since I was the head of strategic thinking. I knew instantly that the King was not in agreement with the ideas presented, and that he was even more amazed that I supposedly was. I could not be an unwitting accomplice to the Evil Prince's scheme, designed to gain the King's support by using my supposed endorsement.

"I am not quite in agreement," I said. Then with as much tact as I could manage, I outlined areas that I thought could be "strengthened" in a way that did not damage the Evil Prince. I made no accusations of what he had done, but I did toss in some of the ideas that the team generated the day before. The King smiled, agreed with my assessment, and left for other meetings.

I cornered the Evil Prince after the meeting, and explained my displeasure that he would put the team in such a compromised position, lying to the King that the ideas were a result of a consensus when they were not and using our authority to gain more for himself. He was caught, so amazingly so, that I realized something else as well. Though his title made him a Prince, he was still an Ogre, with intelligence so scarce that he would put himself in a situation that immediately undermined his own power with both the team and the King. He lasted less than a year, I recall, and then went to kingdoms unknown.

THE COMPETITOR WITHIN

The ancient text, *The Art of War*, written by the Chinese military strategist Sun Tzu around 500 B.C. is truly a masterpiece. He rightly claimed, "War is a matter of vital importance to the State; the province of life and death; the road to survival or ruin. It is mandatory that it be thoroughly studied."

Interestingly, his teachings have not only influenced military strategy for centuries, but have also influenced many less deadly professions as well, including the business world. Sun Tzu suggests that an enemy be attacked where it is weakest, not where it is strongest. "When he concentrates, prepare against him; where he is strong, avoid him. Attack where he is unprepared; sally out when he does not expect you." Those simple strategies are standards in many business texts.

However, there is one teaching from *The Art of War* that, unfortunately, has had too big an impact on too many of today's business people. It is this: "All warfare," says Sun Tzu, "is based upon deception." That is actually a very smart point when applied honestly, and legally, to outwit a competitor in the marketplace. The problem rises when professionals use that strategy *to deceive their own teammates in an attempt to rise to the next level within an organization*. Some concentrate too readily on their competition in the next office, down the hall, or on the next floor.

These are the competitors within. They see you as the competition, although they are supposedly your teammates. While their *public* quest appears to be to beat a competitive company or brand in the marketplace, their *private* quest is to beat you for the next promotion. That is their true end and they will form teams and alliances to do just that.

Once upon a time, two generals within the same company had considerable power, each yearned to have even greater power, and just perhaps, to be the new leader when the day came. Each knew that the other was under consideration for the role. Each acted as if the other general was a competitor although they were in the same kingdom. Camps formed around each of these generals. Some people in the company lined up behind one or the other out of loyalty.

Out of sheer brilliance or stupidity (it was the latter) I kept out of the battles, went about my business, and did whatever was asked of me. That is all I could do, for at the time I was not an officer of any sort, and was far outranked by both generals. I was a newly minted department head, struggling to make that work. I did hear people in each camp say disparaging things about the other. Although I would not truly characterize the comments as duplicitous, their intent was to denigrate the character of the other, and that, I think, is duplicitous when compared with the corporate intent, which is for all to work for the benefit of the whole. However, I kept out of it because the precious energy I had was consumed by my departmental responsibilities. Looking back, I'm very happy that I didn't have extra time on my hands.

When it came time to make company-wide promotions, the Monarch and these two generals met to decide which people in the company were worthy of promotion. A source that attended the meeting told me that the two generals argued over virtually every nominee, because each nominee was in the other's camp. However, when my name was submitted, both generals instantly agreed that I should be an officer, and I'm told surprised each other in doing so. I was thought to be in each camp, I suppose, and I suppose that I was. I wasn't trying to be a double agent. I simply worked like a dog to support the business requests of each camp, while steering away from the politics that engulfed both camps. I kept my head above it, not because I was politically astute, but because I was politically oblivious and stretched too thin to get involved.

After a time, both generals left the company and went to other kingdoms. I could not help but think their internal competitiveness was part of the reason. Both are doing well, from what I understand. Please notice that I never called either general an Evil Baron. To this day, I still admire both of them, and I learned a lot from them. Both are very talented. From my perspective, however, each one had a blind spot; they unfortunately treated the other more as a competitor than as a teammate. I'm sure they both can recite reasons why, but regardless of the list of grievances, their actions had unfortunate consequences.

Of course, companies can benefit greatly from the right kind of internal competitiveness, such as bestowing rewards upon the salesperson that beats all others in annual sales contests. This is positive, for the competitiveness helps achieve corporate ends. The problem arises when the competitiveness is undertaken to achieve selfish ends alone, for then corporate objectives are at risk.

TAKING CREDIT NOT DUE YOU

It is simply not right to take more credit than is due to you for work others do, either on purpose or inadvertently. Nor is it right to hide hard-working serfs under a bushel of wheat when the King approaches. In effect, it is a form of deception. The following are three stories, each with increasing consequences of taking credit not due. The first is a small incident that happened years ago in a well-known company. The incident provided more entertainment than harm. Still, it is a story about how a junior executive who contributed the most got the least credit.

Anonymous Storyteller

I had been working on a brand study for my client for 18 months. The scope of the project was large, and we developed many findings and recommendations. We worked 24/7 in the last six months of the project to get it ready to present to the most senior management of the client's company. When it came time to do the presentation, my big boss told my direct boss that she was the one who should do the presentation, which I totally understood, but that I could still go to the meeting. The presentation included a written document, as well as visual elements propped up on an easel, and a videotape. When we got to the meeting, the big boss said he had a way for me to participate more directly. I was thrilled until I found out what I would be doing. My job was to stand in front of the easels and pull off the black cloths that were hiding the displays underneath, á la Vanna White. Now I am an educated person, who killed herself working on a complex project and I ended up presenting myself to senior management as a spokes model. I was not happy. After I uncovered all the easels, the big boss whispers to me, "Now run down and stand in front of the VCR until the chairman decides he wants to see the video and then you hit the ON button, do you understand?" (Just when you think it cannot get worse, it does.) So, I did as directed and proceeded to stand in front of the VCR, doing my best Vanna White imitation while my direct boss presented the study. Several senior executives with whom I had worked extensively were in the room too, and were shaking their heads in acknowledgment, feeling "my pain." Anyway, the chairman decides it's time to see the video and I couldn't help myself. I swung my arms around as the models do on The Price Is Right, pointed dramatically at the VCR, and hit the ON button with great flourish. One of the other executives practically fell on the floor he was laughing so hard, the chairman looked at me somewhat perplexed, and my big boss was fuming. I made my point and the big boss never asked me to do something like that again!

The person in this last story is rather senior today, and so the incident was of no immediate harm, though stealing an opportunity for a junior employee to shine is shameful. The next story tells the tale of a Good Knight caught in a moral dilemma, all because a more senior associate decided to take credit not due to him. The potential consequences are greater.

Anonymous Storyteller

As a new faculty member in a medical school, I was given a copy of the lecture that the dean of the medical school had delivered at a prestigious European university. (I received it because it was on a topic in my area of expertise and it was believed that it would interest me). As I read it, however, it seemed very familiar. When I looked in a book on the subject, I found that the entire lecture had been created using sentences (sometimes slightly rearranged) from this book. There was virtually nothing in the lecture not taken directly from the book in question. I was in a quandary. This was clearly plagiarism, but what was my responsibility? What would happen if this oral presentation were to be published? Did I have the chance to prevent further embarrassment and wrongdoing? But as a junior, newly hired faculty member, would saying something jeopardize my career?

I did go to my department chairman, who was clearly not pleased by my discovery.

The final story of this trilogy is more tragic still. Yet the roots of the issue are the same; taking credit (and in this case actual business) not due to you.

Anonymous Storyteller

I once had a boss who had over several years become my best friend. We had different backgrounds and skill sets, and learned a lot from each other. I videotaped his wedding. As the tech sector in which we worked grew hotter, my projects suddenly began to find greater commercial acceptance than the ones he initiated. This shouldn't have been a problem for him since he was getting credit for my work, but it became especially troubling on one particular occasion when we both went to corporate to pitch separate projects, one that I had been working on for more than two years and one that he had been working on for less than two weeks. No surprise, mine was approved to go into production and his was not. A few days later, corporate leaked word of my project and one of the three national news anchors called our office for an interview with me about it.

I never got the message. My boss picked it up from our receptionist. When corporate called me a few days later to prepare me for the interview, I asked, "What interview?" I then went to my boss/best friend and asked him about it. "I've been meaning to talk to you about that," he said, "I don't think you are the right person to run that project." I was aghast. Of course, he was the right person to run my project, because he did not have a project to run and an anchor from the national news was interested in it.

I appealed to corporate but they stood by the chain of command and told me to work on one of my other projects. I suggested that might be fine, save for the fact that I had two years in this one and there was no way my boss could pull it off in the same time frame without destroying it. The learning alone would take him a year and they wanted it done in a year. Not wishing to see my idea die a slow death and then be hung later for the concept, I returned a call to a start-up that had been contacting me for many months. Totally depressed by the loss of what should have been the most important project of my career, I got an offer, took it, and relocated. What followed was the seven best years of my career, both creatively and financially. No question, no contest.

The friendship ended, my former boss created a disaster. The project was completed more than three years later at many times the budget I forecast and resulted in almost no revenue for the company. He was fired; our division was closed. That year my team at the new company won a record number of industry achievement awards, and our company's stock quadrupled. I was promoted to VP that year.

I no longer have best friends at work.

A NATURAL TENDENCY

Most of us lie, according to the experts. It appears to be a natural part of social interaction. One study by psychologist Robert Feldman videotaped 121 pairs of graduate students as they greeted others they did not know. They were not told the study was about honesty. In the course of being introduced to others and making small talk, 60 percent of the graduate students lied at least once during the 10-minute conversation. The graduates told an average of two to three lies during these scant 10 minutes! Who caught them? The graduates caught themselves, when, after the session, they were asked to review the tape for inaccuracies. Interestingly, the graduates did not think they said anything untruthful until they went back and viewed the tapes. If they can lie in a short 10-minute discussion and not know it, think about each 10 minutes you work, day in and day out, over the course of an entire year. How many lies have you told that you didn't even recognize as lies?

Why do we lie? The study revealed that men tend to lie to make themselves look good. Women tend to lie to make those they are talking to feel better. Both can have drastic, not always positive, consequences when put in the context of vying for raises, sales, promotions, or trying to influence employees, compensation committees, the board of directors, shareholders, or the federal government.

We must be ever-vigilant, not just in recognizing the deceptive practices of others, but our own as well.

A Knight's Code of Business

Truthfulness: A Good Knight is honest, keeps promises, and does not get involved with duplicity of any kind, grand or subtle.

And Other Advice

Good Knights, beware, as there are *occasionally* those who seek to fool you into believing they are Good Knights also. You may meet only a couple of them in your entire career, but they can be devastating. Trust is built upon deeds, not upon words or appearances. You can often tell an Evil Baron by the Ogres and Henchmen they employ. But at times, Evil Barons will reveal themselves by being caught in their own deceptions. Once you know them for what they are, never let them gain the ear of the monarch. Bring important controversies into the light so that fairness can be re-established. This will greatly lessen the evil doer's effect upon the kingdom.

Good Squires-in-Training, stay clear of politics. It will consume you. Better to concentrate on your tasks. Never, ever do battle with an Evil Baron, for you will be squashed. You have neither the strength nor experience to win. Enlist the aid of a Good Knight. You might be able to take on an Ogre or two, and reveal them for that they are. It is good training for when you rise within the Kingdom.

Good Monarchs, beware of the motives of those beneath you, and those you hire, for there are *occasional* changelings about who can blind you to their evil intent while poisoning you against those who are truly good. They are few, so there is no reason to be paranoid. You can often detect those few early, for those who consistently use deception to get ahead often leave a trail of bruised and battered executives at past jobs. You simply have to check thoroughly.

Evil Barons, Henchman and Ogres, what you do not know is that many times others can see your deceptive ways. Why? Because the falsehoods you manufacture often reach the attention of those who know better, and the promises you break eventually claim the attention of many. So keep up your deceptions, keep demonstrating your lack of integrity, as it is the best way we can identify you.

Chapter 4

Fraud, Larceny, and other Evils

*"Out, malicious enchanters! Away, hoggish scum! I am Don
Quixote of La Mancha, against whom your vile intentions are
of no avail."*

—Don Quixote

In this corporate kingdom there are shades of evil; some are small
and relatively harmless, others are grand and devastating. While aristocrats often feel *entitled* instead of *grateful*, and those who are duplicitous use *deception* to achieve *selfish ends*, others go one step further and
conduct themselves in ways that they run afoul of the law. They steal
from their companies, they steal from their fellow executives, they steal
from shareholders, and they rob employees of their jobs because of
their profound greed. Those at the highest level of management sometimes come to see themselves as above society's laws, and above respect
for other's property.

When I began writing this book, there were few stories about high-
level executives involved in white-collar crime. However, in 2002, it
seems that corporate America decided, en masse, to help fill in the pages
of this particular chapter. I should be grateful, I suppose, that those who
commit corporate shenanigans have decided to reveal themselves at this
opportune time. The news accounts have been so prolific, in fact, that
many newspapers and magazines have created charts to help us keep
track of the incidents and the players. It is a daunting task. Here, para-
phrased, is what the *Los Angeles Times* reported on the front page of its
business section on June 27, 2002.

WorldCom: MCI's parent company reported that it had inflated profit. It improperly accounted for $3.9 billion in routine expenses. (Subsequent to the *Times* article, WorldCom filed for bankruptcy, which is ironic in light of the fact that earlier, the chief executive said that WorldCom was too big to fail. We can add arrogance to their liberal accounting practices.)

Enron: It filed for bankruptcy protection in December 2001. It apparently used off-balance-sheet deals to keep billions of dollars in debt off the books.

Arthur Andersen: The accounting firm, whose clients included Enron and WorldCom, was convicted on obstruction of justice charges for its handling of Enron's accounting.

Tyco International: Ex-CEO L. Dennis Kozlowski was charged with evading more than $1 million in New York State and city sales taxes.

Adelphia Communications: Filed for bankruptcy protection. The government is investigating questionable financial transactions, including $3 billion in off-the-books loans to the founding Rigas family. (Subsequent to the *Times* article, members of the Rigas family were arrested for fraud, accused of using company funds for personal use.)

Global Crossing: The telecommunications company is being investigated by two congressional committees and others to determine if it used fraudulent transactions to inflate revenue.

ImClone: Chief executive Samuel D. Waksal resigned and was arrested on insider trading charges for allegedly tipping off family members to the company's poor prospects. Martha Stewart, a friend of Waksal's, is under scrutiny for selling her stock before the decline, suggesting that she benefited from insider knowledge.

Thank you, the *Los Angeles Times*. It is hard to keep track of all the corruption, but you, along with *The Wall Street Journal, The New York Times, USA Today,* and many others, are doing a great job!

I do not know how all of these cases will be resolved, who will be cleared and who will not, who will get a slap on the wrist and who will go to jail for a very long time, but I'll make some observations.

INNOVATIVE EVIL BARONS

The people who commit these types of scams are innovative. After all, they were smart to begin with. Some executives have classified ordinary expenses as long-term capital expenses so they don't have to immediately deduct the expenses as a cost of doing business, making the firms look more profitable in the short term, and the stock more attractive. Executives are playing a shell game, creating outside partnerships whose losses never make it to the parent company's balance sheets until it is too late. Executives aren't paying sales taxes on personal items. Executives are giving family and friends inside information about the company's future success or woes, thus tipping them off about when they should buy or sell stock.

Here is an old story: David Thatcher, past president of a company called Critical Path, allegedly committed fraud by convincing an ex-colleague to sign a contract for $2 million dollars of Critical Path's software so that the company could make its sales goals, keep Wall Street happy, and push the price of the stock up. The contract was, of course, bogus. This was the same scheme that allegedly went on at HPL Technologies Inc. It had to warn investors that its financial statement might not be trustworthy because of apparently bogus transactions made by a former chief executive. Then there is Alan Bond. He was a well-known money manager. As I write this, he is currently under indictment for directing over $50 million in unprofitable trades into his clients' accounts, and profitable ones into his own account, so reported *The Wall Street Journal.* With all of his accounts now frozen, he must use a public defender to represent him in court. There is some justice in that. Alan Bond has an ideal pedigree, having graduated from both Dartmouth College and Harvard Business School. However, college degrees do not fix personality flaws (assuming the allegations are true). While it is reported that he never made more than $350,000 a year, he had far more than that in credit card bills. More interesting, was that

Mr. Bond had a bumpy road along his career path, but people hired him anyway. Either they did not check his past thoroughly enough, or they didn't check it at all.

THUGS ARE THUGS

People who actually perpetrate such acts are common thugs. It is sometimes hard to realize that, because it is hard to get past the white collars, the good colleges, the mansions, and the executive status, but they are thugs. We typically think of thugs as sleazy, low-class types hiding in alleys. However, who is the bigger thug, the guy who steals from one person at a time, or the guy who steals from millions of people at a time? The only difference is that the executive found a bigger bank and more of us to rob.

Most senior executives who steal probably do not consider themselves to be thugs, or that they are stealing. Why? Let us review: first, they feel *entitled* because of their position. They begin to grab more, taxing the whole organization in ways that they believe are justified by their services. Then gradually, and not so gradually, they begin to use *duplicity* as they climb the corporate ladder. Then, at some point, they cross a line, and many times, do not realize that they have crossed a line. Why? Because they are *entitled!* The line is for others, not for them. Do you see the circular logic to it all? Entitlement. Greed. Duplicity. Illegality. The data that connects these dots are right before our eyes. The *Los Angeles Times* recently reported that the "top officers of 23 major companies currently under investigation for accounting irregularities were paid 70 percent more than the average chief executive officer of a large U.S. company," based upon a study by a nonprofit advocacy group.

BusinessWeek noted that while the stock market lost 6.8 percent of its value shortly following September 11, 2001 attacks on the World Trade Center, it lost 18 percent of its value shortly following corporate scandals. Hence, scandals from within contributed to greater financial losses than did attacks from foreign parties. It affects all of us, particularly since over 50 percent of us own stock. You may feel far removed from Enron, but we are as close to it as our last pension statement.

Here is an insight that was reported in *USA Today* from a golfing survey conducted by Starwood Hotels & Resorts. Eighty-two percent of CEOs state that they undercount their strokes, improve their lie, and so forth. That means they cheat. However, when asked in a separate question if they are honest at golf, 99 percent said yes (remember the duplicity chapter). They actually admit to the methods of cheating, but not to cheating itself. They *excuse away* their own actions. It gets better. *USA Today* went on to report that of these executives, "67 percent believe that a person who cheats at golf would probably cheat at business." Get it? They can see the human weakness that envelopes others that can lead to illegality, but they refuse to accept that it envelopes them. Power is seductive. We know this. However, those who are caught up in it do not always realize that they are caught in a vortex. Some have become so used to aristocratic treatment that they think they are above the rules of mere mortals (you and me).

DYSFUNCTIONAL EVIL BARONS

None of this is new; it has just gotten BIGGER. The most evil Barons have revealed themselves to us by destroying their companies with tactics that appear illegal (I still have to use the word "alleged"). In large measure, that is because the Evil Barons who have been involved in some of these instances have become incompetent and hence, dysfunctional as Evil Barons.

This requires an explanation. Let's refer back to Exhibit 1 on page 24. Ever-shrewd Evil Barons exist in the upper right hand quadrant D (Very competent/experienced yet with low moral tendencies). But the Evil Barons who have gotten caught recently have demonstrated amazing incompetence, allowing their insatiable desire for more wealth and success to make them stupid. It blinded them to common sense and sound management practices, and resulted in such mismanagement that they killed the company that fed them. They were dysfunctional even as Evil Barons. True Evil Barons do not destroy their companies. Let me repeat that for any Evil Baron who is reading this: *True Evil Barons do not destroy their companies.* That flies in the face of competence. Even nature's parasites know that they have to keep their host alive, or they die as well. Looking at today's headlines, it is clear that some of these Evil Barons don't deserve such an exulted title, as they are too stupid to know that, for clarification, *True Evil Barons do not destroy their companies.* They keep them alive so that they can continue to plunder. These guys are an insult to True Evil Barons everywhere. In fact, when some executives at Enron recognized the effect of their incompetence, they took one more swipe at their host company to gain as much feed as possible while the company was in its death throes. Am I off base on this, or were these guys dysfunctional and greedy right to the very end? The authors of the book *The 22 Immutable Laws of Marketing* point out that "Success often leads to arrogance, and arrogance to failure." Does this sound familiar?

Such antics hurt us all. As I write this, the stock market continues to fall because investors have come to believe that all books must be cooked. Shareholders, those invested in pension funds, and those laid off, are all suffering due to a super class of dysfunctional Evil Barons. Here is my question. The federal government is identifying those companies whose Evil Barons became dysfunctional. That is because these Evil Barons were the ones that *identified themselves* by destroying their host companies. What of all the Evil Barons who are competent in their evil? Who's finding them? Answer: no one. They are smart enough not to get caught. I do not endorse their antics, but at least they know how to keep thousands of people employed.

THE PIRATE NEXT DOOR

The grand stories that make the headlines can make evil feel very far away (unless you worked for Enron). For most of us, there is a distance that makes us create a mental barrier between them and us (even as we review our declining pension statements), so we become a bit naïve when it comes to our own worlds and day-to-day business dealings.

SURVEY OF 100

Only 3 percent agreed (completely or somewhat) that they know of people within their company who have committed a significant illegal act to benefit themselves or the company.

Those numbers are good. It means either that such crime is rare, or that employees who have committed such acts have yet to be caught. When they are, it can be a jolt to one's sense of fair play and honesty.

Some years ago, a piece of my Pollyanna sensibility was stripped away and I lost a bit of my own naïveté. I was working for a client, doing research, discovering consumer insights and using them to craft motivating brand messages and advertising. I worked directly with both the client's marketing director and the head of research. All went well. We worked side by side in many instances, and I felt a connection. Moreover, the advertising we developed was brilliant, having not only tested well in research, but in the marketplace as well. Each of us was rewarded with the belief that the company was prospering because of our efforts, and there was every reason to believe that those efforts would pay off in personal ways as well via subsequent paychecks, raises, and promotions.

However, one among us desired a bit more. The marketing director called and asked that I join him for a meeting. He would not tell me the subject over the telephone, only that we had to talk, and that it was of some urgency. I arrived at his office, notebook in hand, eager to learn about some new product or service that only I was entrusted to hear about. Instead, as I waited with my pen poised over my pad, the marketing director began to speak with words and sentences I had never heard first hand.

The research director had been caught stealing. He was apparently benefiting from money he was sending to outside research suppliers. I never got the full details. He was participating in one of several possible scams: getting kickbacks from legitimate companies; employing his buddies who were conducting the research for him; conducting the research himself and taking the cash; or not conducting the research at all, but pretending to and having the money diverted to him.

I was dumbfounded. "What?" I kept on saying, unwilling to believe that this guy, whom I had known for months and who had seemed to be a reasonable and fair man, could be the same one who would have conducted such a scheme. The marketing director was equally shocked, for he was as naïve as I. But a deep background check revealed that this research director had previous convictions that were not detected when he was first hired.

The marketing director asked me to investigate the status of all research projects, contact the research houses to ascertain which were legitimate and which were not, and to help the various divisions of this company get their research projects moving forward, legitimately. For several days, I played triage for well over a dozen projects, and I eventually got them all on track.

This man was an evil Henchman, too incompetent to stay hidden. I guess it is good that incompetence and low character are often bedfellows. Here are a couple of stories that would leave most of us scratching our heads in bewilderment.

Anonymous Storyteller

An operations manager approved numerous bills for painting of the office. The painter turned out to be his roommate, with the payments made to his home address. It gets worse. The office is "painted" over 30 times on paper, but only once in three years in reality. How did this come to light? The operations manager brought the roommate to a company party and introduced him to work associates. An assistant, processing payments the following week, remembered the name and made the connection. The operations manager was fired. The assistant was promoted.

Anonymous Storyteller

When I worked at a multi-national company, I witnessed one of the most flagrant acts of larceny—and stupidity—in my business career. One of my employees (23 years old, well educated, and whose family was very rich) had gained access to some blank company checks, and had forged my signature on a check in the amount of approximately $10,000, made payable to himself. Fortunately, another one of my employees detected the forgery during the monthly bank reconciliation process and brought the matter directly to my attention.

Once the facts were presented to me, I was both outraged (over someone trying to take advantage of me and the company) and disappointed (the employee was a rising star in my department).

With the concrete facts in hand, it was time to notify key com-
pany officials, and the (thief) employee. The company's attorney told
me to contact the police, and have him immediately arrested. I elected
not to contact the police, but decided to "put the fear of God" into the
employee by addressing the forgery directly with him.

The employee admitted to forging my signature, and explained
that the money was used to invest in a "drug" deal in which he would
lend $10,000 to a friend and the friend would double his investment
by returning $20,000 to my employee. The employee stated, in turn,
he would return the money to the company before anyone had dis-
covered the funds had been missing.

After threatening to contact the police, and notifying his family, I
informed the employee that he had six hours to return the money or
the authorities would be contacted. The money was returned within
six hours, and the employee was terminated without further incident.
Today, this person has risen to the rank of a senior officer in a major
company and continues to thank me for not ruining his business career
by prosecuting him.

It is hard to place yourself in someone else's shoes, but I probably
would have prosecuted. I hate the thought of letting a shady character
get away at a lower level, only to rise to the next level where the loot
will be greater. These types of incidents may be more common than we
think, because when such events occur, companies can be quite good
at keeping them quiet.

MOMENTS OF TRUTH

These are moments of truth for any Good Knight. There is nothing
more frightening, or that requires more bravery, than when an executive discovers he or she must blow the whistle on his own company.
When company interests run afoul of society's interests and the law,
one must decide for the benefit of the greater good. This can be devastating for those who step up, lance in hand, to follow a higher call-
ing. Few of us have such courage, for it is not an easy task to take on
one's own King.

Douglas Durand once worked for TAP Pharmaceuticals Products, Inc., as vice president of sales. He took the brave step of filing a lawsuit that claimed that the company had encouraged urologists to prescribe its prostate cancer drug, Lupron, by offering kickbacks. Investigated by the government, TAP eventually agreed to pay $560 million to settle civil claims and an additional $290 million in criminal fines according to a report in *People* magazine. It took grit for this Knight to right a wrong. But Durand was luckier than most Knights who do the same. He collected $79 million of the civil settlement.

Some apparent Knights have a very tough go at it. As I write this, David B. Duncan is in a predicament. He was an accountant for Arthur Andersen during the Enron collapse. He testified, under oath, that he not only destroyed Enron documents, but that he knew that his actions were illegal at the time. He pleaded guilty. Then the unbelievable happened. While a jury found Arthur Andersen guilty of obstruction of justice, the jurors said it was not due to David Duncan's actions. Instead, the jury found a lawyer at Andersen guilty of misdoing, so David Duncan stepped up and declared to have done wrong, and yet the jury looked elsewhere. Who will hire him now?

Knighthood can be a tough business. You must be sure of accusations you make, and even once confirmed, you will struggle with the decision to act. There is no easy answer, although those who take such a brave step will ultimately make the organization and society better in the end.

A NEAR MISS (I THINK)

In all my years in business, including 17 years in an advertising agency, I have never been at a meeting where someone said or inferred with a wink, "Hey, let's do some shady stuff and get rich." Never. Now, I might be one of those executives who simply does not know that he has already crossed dozens of lines. However, assuming that I'm not, let me tell you a story of a line I did recognize. If it was crossed, nobody would have been the wiser. Our agency had just completed the production of a television commercial. Lawyers for the client and the agency raised the concern that the commercial might mislead consumers into believing the product did something that it could not actually do. This would put us in violation of a host of laws, including regulations of the FTC. Not a good thing. As the research director of the agency, I was asked to put together a research study designed to determine if consumers were, in fact, mislead. With the client's research director and lawyers looking over my shoulder every moment, I began. This was big stuff; both moral principle and millions of dollars were at stake.

When we were content with the research design, and felt the test would hold up to scrutiny if challenged, we conducted the study. The research showed that *a small percentage* of consumers were confused to the point that it might be considered misleading. Not great. With results in hand, I made my way to the client's building, jetted up to the executive floor, and headed to the CEO's office. I was greeted by the client researcher, who wished me luck and then vanished. I mean disappeared! Gone! Adios! Catlike instincts told this person that a storm was ready to break. I entered the CEO's office and sat alongside one lawyer, an agency guy who headed the account, and the head of marketing. No one was smiling. They knew my news was bad.

Sitting there, I suddenly wondered what would happen if the CEO heard the results and then decided to run the commercial anyway. I wondered if I would have the courage to object, and possibly to lose my job in the process. I felt sweat begin to drip from my underarms, down my body, and into my socks. Not my day.

The CEO entered, sat, and was all business. "What are the results?"

I passed a one-page note around the table and explained that we were *a couple percentage points over the line.* I got a hard stare. "Not good," I thought. Either the research method will be challenged, or the results, or the desire to do the right thing. Something's going to give.

"Well," said this Monarch on this particular day. "How do we make the commercial so it doesn't confuse them?"

"Whoa," thought I. "A near miss!" To this very day, I believe that if this Monarch had been a different one, it could have gone the other way. No one would have known, and I would have been put in a situation where my moral compass would have been greatly challenged. We spent 15 minutes discussing how the commercial could be corrected in order to ensure better comprehension. We spent significant dollars to make the changes to the commercial, and the spot aired. I am glad that all of us that day just wanted to do the right thing, even though no one knew about it, and I greatly admire those who have to face the opposite, and choose the noble path.

IT BEGINS AT THE BEGINNING

We don't always hire well. People with a bent for illegality are many times a tad shady to begin with. They cut the same corners in high school that they do in the boardroom. Maybe I'm jaded, but having worked with so many people over decades, I have never, ever seen a personality flaw get fixed. Maybe some of those flaws were a result of nature (genetics), perhaps some of it was nurture (upbringing), but it is not really the job of business to try to sort out why a certain person's moral compass is what it is. It is simply what it is.

While companies cannot always hire angels, many of them have to try harder. Some companies do not check items as simple as schools from which candidates claim to have graduated. Some don't bother checking all of the past employers. *Time* magazine reported on a study from one of the nation's top executive search firms that revealed, "23 percent of 7,000 resumes submitted for president, VP and board-of-director positions have been at least a little cooked." Another study reported in *Newsweek* revealed, "44 percent of employment records show a discrepancy between information an applicant provides and what a past employer reports."

Even when we hire well, we must be constantly vigilant. For many decisions enter gray areas so that we can have difficulty distinguishing when gray turns to black. Even the very best of Knights can have their moral compasses fail them after a time, which is why it is best that each of us routinely checks in with those we trust.

AND IT ENDS AT THE END

Here's what many experts say should be done to help reduce the enticements that lead to white-collar crime:

Executives who are suspected of wrongdoing must go to trial, and if found guilty, must be punished to the full extent of the law. Some want to confiscate assets of those convicted, and redistribute them to those whose assets were stolen.

Accounting firms should not provide consulting services to companies they audit. Independent oversight boards should have the authority to review and investigate corporations' books, and act if need be.

Companies need to institute codes of ethics and actually require their employees to READ them, and to conduct formal training programs.

Executive compensation should be scrutinized harder, especially where stock options are concerned because such incentives are not listed as expenses on income statements, which leads to all sorts of misadventures, illegal and otherwise.

President Bush announced his own proposal on July 9, 2002. Although some analysts felt that his suggestions were weak, eventually, mud wrestling with Congress and the courts and the President will produce some reform. As I write this, Congress has just passed measures that are aimed at eliminating deceptive accounting and management practices while increasing penalties and making CEOs more responsible for their company's financial reports. However, crooks are innovative and the greatest danger we face is ultimate indifference that might return when the current furor lessens and we go about our business as usual. Evil Barons will still be Evil Barons. New regulations may serve to lessen the plundering and uncover the more incompetent Evil Barons, and that is good. However, employees must remain aware at all levels, with a *code* that they can refer to and live by.

Moreover, when we are done cleaning up business, let's clean up government. We can start with all of the false campaign advertising that never, ever seems to be brought under the scrutiny of . . . well . . . government. Someone else can write that book.

A Knight's Code of Business

Law Abiding: A Good Knight abides by laws of man and morality.

And Other Advice

Good Knights, do deep background checks of potential employees. One executive told me that we often spend more dollars inspecting a house we plan to buy for faults and repairs, than we do checking out a senior person we plan to hire. The hardest thing a Knight must do is battle with his or her King in order to achieve greater ends, for societal interests outweigh company interests. Above all things, be sure you are right, *for legal standards are not for the novice to interpret.* If you do challenge the King, and things do not go well, you may be immediately banished, and other Kings will be hesitant to hire you, but you will know in your heart that you are a Good Knight. Take comfort in that.

Good Squires-in-Training, do not be enticed to do an Evil Baron's illegal bidding. Leave the company before you become a conspirator. Character transcends everything (I know, it sounds preachy, but it is nevertheless true).

Good Monarchs, investigate infractions of current employees quickly. It is better for a kingdom to clean its own house than to be subjected to the federal kingdom that will do it for you. It also sets a positive example for the kingdom at large.

Evil Monarchs and Barons, eventually, the more incompetent ones among your breed will be caught. How stupid you must be to destroy your own company, the host that fed you. It is better for you to use sound and legitimate management principles and let the company thrive, for its decay and destruction will serve to bring unwanted attention (that's when law enforcement will nail you).

Chapter 5

Indecency

"Do not appear covetous (even if you are so, which I do not believe) or given to women and gluttony, for if the people and those who deal with you get to know of your prevailing tendency, they will open a barrage of fire on you on that side until they have brought you down to the depths of perdition."

—Don Quixote

$\sim$

THE STORY OF HANK

There was once an executive named Hank. He was extremely well educated, and did much for his kingdom. In fact, after Hank became CEO, he made his organization far more powerful than it had been before his arrival. He helped it achieve world status by turning it into a truly global competitor. Hank was a shrewd guy. Yes, he was brutal to his competitors sometimes, but that is what was required in the industry in which his organization thrived. But Hank had a weakness. He couldn't keep his hands off the ladies. This grew into a character flaw. Moreover, in many ways, it prevented Hank from achieving even more.

Soon after Hank became CEO, he married a lovely woman by the name of Catherine. Things went well for a time, but after a while, Hank started chasing another lady at work. It was an office romance. Her name was Anne and she was, indeed, lovely. So Hank eventually divorced his first wife and married Anne. Things went well for a while, until he got bored again. Worse yet, it seems that Anne began to have an affair of her own with someone else at the office. It was a pretty happening place. The CEO wasn't all that happy. So Hank cast Anne aside and began to have an affair with someone else, and then someone else, and then someone else. And so it went for Hank, with ex-wife after ex-wife piling up.

Do you know someone like this at work? Someone who might be very capable in business, but all anyone talks about is his or her wild side? It is unfortunate, but for those around the water cooler, that's entertainment. Rather than speak of all of Hank's accomplishments, the organization was always abuzz with tales of Hank's liaisons. They talked about Hank at luncheons, on breaks, at company picnics where executives would bring their families and play all sorts of games. Every time Hank walked by with his new romance, employees spoke in whispers. In fact, they spent an inordinate amount of time talking about Hank's affairs, and the organization even had to devote resources in defense of many of them. The time and resources could have been spent in other more worthy company pursuits.

Hank didn't care what people said. This CEO felt pretty entitled. Power does that. In all, Hank went through six wives that he met on the job. He divorced a couple of them, and executed others. That's right, he executed them. While this rather talented man did much for his organization—his England—most of us remember him for his wild lifestyle. Henry VIII took over the throne of England in 1509 and died in 1547. His last wife, another Catherine, outlived him. Good for her.

Henry VIII is an extreme example of entitlement, for no one could stand before his decrees, not even the Church of England or the Pope, both formidable powers. There are many Henry VIIIs in business today. Some are very close to being Philosopher Kings in character and competence, but a character flaw (seeds of indecency of one sort or another) prevents them from leaving a truly lasting and powerful legacy. They invite problems. They are arrogant. They feel entitled and their actions end up fanning the flames of gossip, undermining their ability to rule, and to leave an honorable legacy.

"I didn't have sexual relations with that woman, Miss Lewinsky," said former President Bill Clinton. No matter what his accomplishments, that sentence will follow him always. He lied, and the country and his staff spent an inordinate amount of time and resources on the issue, which could have been spent for a far greater good.

Harrassment takes this one step further. C. Michael Greene, former president of the Grammy Music Awards, resigned amidst questions of sexual harassment. The organization paid a former female Grammy executive $650,000 to settle charges, reported the *LA Times*, though Greene declared his innocence. *Forbes* recently ran an article about sexual harassment at the highest levels. It commented, "Typically firms pay but admit no wrongdoing." The accused often denied the charges. The article notes that this was true of Peter Karmanos, chief executive of Compuware, Dan Wassong, chief executive of Del Laboratories, and Sidney Frank, chief executive of Sidney Frank Importers. Each of these three companies paid significant sums to settle the cases. Each of the three executives kept his job.

While it is certainly the case that some sexual harassment charges are bogus, others are not. Still others are never brought to light and that's an even bigger problem. Let's look at some numbers. The Equal Employment Opportunity Commission receives approximately 15,000 new sexual harassment cases each year. Yet the incidence of sexual harassment appears to be far more prevalent than the actual numbers who decide to sue. A 1995 survey found that 44 percent of women and 19 percent of men claim to have experienced some form of unwanted sexual attention during the previous two years. That means many millions of cases that are never reported.

The current size of financial settlements across the United States is estimated at $53 million a year. One California attorney's website announces that the average sexual harassment verdict in the state from 1989 to 1997 was about $275,000, and that the average cost to defend against such a suit was about $300,000. This does not include other costs, such as higher turnover of able employees or costs associated with decreased productivity.

APPEARANCES ARE TRUTHS

One survey showed that 80 percent of workers either know of or have been involved in an office romance. This seems only natural, since that is where we spend a great deal of our time.

Problems can arise even when such romances are pure in their motivation and actions, *but are not construed as such by those on the outside.* That is one of the most difficult things that all Good Knights must learn. Appearances are truths to those looking in. The most noble of actions will be misconstrued. Good Knights have to be ever mindful of how their actions might appear to those on the outside. Such romances, even the noblest ones, can sully reputations. A woman who gets a well-deserved promotion will not necessarily be thought to have gained it fairly if she had an affair with the boss. A man who is fired will believe it was related to his spurning the affections of a supervisor, although it was due to his own poor performance. Among those who are looking at the royal court from afar, untruths are more titillating to believe and more comforting to believe if you are the person supposedly wronged. Such is human nature.

Knights must be ever vigilant of these perceptions. You cannot stop your own affairs of the heart, but you should not become suddenly oblivious to the perceptions of those around you either. To reiterate the caution of our friend Don Quixote, " . . . *for if the people and those who deal with you get to know of your prevailing tendency, they will open a barrage of fire on you . . ."*

Office romances may, even inadvertently, affect a company's effectiveness in unsuspecting, subtle ways.

 SURVEY OF 100

Fourteen percent know of people who have had a romance with a co-worker or subordinate, which impeded the smooth operation of the department or company business.

A TANGLED MESS

Here's a story that shows just how tangled situations can become, and yet it is far too common.

Anonymous Storyteller

One of our divisional heads has a history with women. Maybe it's because Bob is a good-looking guy and a charmer. He married when he was young, but by the time he got to our company he was on his second wife. But it didn't last. Bob had an affair with his secretary. That caused a bit of a ruckus in the office, but it calmed down when he divorced his second wife, married the secretary, and she left the company to be his new wife. Then Bob began flirting with an assistant who worked for one of his managers. That was awkward as it was, but then it got worse. The first indication that they were having an affair occurred when the assistant seemed to know too much about upcoming, top level announcements in the division before anybody else knew. It also happened that Bob suddenly knew too much about what was happening way down in the ranks. People began to tiptoe around the assistant. When layoffs came, no one felt comfortable putting the assistant's name on the list, because it would have to be approved by Bob. Can't even be sure if she deserved to be on the list, but it wasn't about to be discussed. When other people were sacrificed for the sake of layoffs, they cried foul, and then they cried for a lawyer. Was it really discrimination, or just a situation that looked bad because of the complications? The company paid to settle. Virtually everyone associated with the craziness left the company, except Bob.

There are lots of Bobs (and Barbaras). In fact, the previous story was not from just one source, but one I put together from various story-tellers who were all talking about different incidents, different people, and different companies. I was surprised at the similarities—the common themes, the common incidents, and the common outcomes. Some companies, when faced with such incidents, do nothing about it until it is too late, and some do too little even after that. Why? Because some Bobs and Barbaras are so valued by their company for their business skills, the organization overlooks the infractions, repeatedly. It is also difficult to address affairs of the heart, for a good case can be made that such affairs are none of the company's business, unless of course, it affects business, something that can be hard to determine until it's too late.

Knights have to be beyond reproach, as difficult as that may be to achieve. That means not only to strive for decency in all things, but for the appearance of decency as well. It's hard to write those words and not sound like a prude and intruding on personal affairs. However, it is what it is.

DEVILS WEARING HALOS

Let's now consider even more extreme situations. Several female teachers made headlines recently when they allegedly had affairs with their students. One teacher conceived a child (I guess that's no longer "allegedly"). No organization is immune from indecency. In fact, some organizations become fertile grounds for Evil Barons, for the very reason that the organizations appear to be beyond reproach.

I made a point earlier that Evil Barons can appear as Good Knights so they can fool us all. There is no better example of that than those few, with evil intentions, who have infiltrated the Catholic Church. This venerable institution has become embroiled in a multitude of accusations of sexual misconduct by a few of its priests. It is a classic example of people with evil intent, hiding in plain sight and under halos so that they can achieve selfish, and in this case, criminal and deviant ends. What makes this case so amazing is that these particular Evil Barons sought out a place thought to be beyond reproach. It is not all that different from organized-crime families that need a legitimate business in order to launder money, or billionaires who donate huge sums for great causes in order to appease a populous that is leery of their mainstream-business dealings. It all comes from the same place: hide in plain sight, right next to angels so that you bask in the glow and appear to be an angel yourself.

These Evil Barons are very shrewd. They can also have a devastating impact on organizations, particularly organizations that are known to be good. Why? First, because good-hearted organizations have trouble believing that evil has truly infiltrated their ranks. Second, because some organizations are so afraid of scandal (Evil Barons rely on this), that they mismanage the situation in attempts to keep it quiet, causing even greater harm.

It is generally accepted that the Catholic Church did not act fast enough when the first incidents occurred, didn't act at all in some cases, or shuffled the problem from one parish to the next. Its inability to address the problem made matters worse. *BusinessWeek* reported, "Plaintiff's lawyers say as much as $1 billion in settlements, many of them secret, has already been paid since the first big sexual-abuse case surfaced in Louisiana in 1985." If the goal of the church is to bring God into people's lives, to help them deal with earthly miseries, and to prepare them for a life in heaven, that $1 billion could have done a lot of good to help achieve those ends. It gets worse. A Gallup poll in 2002 found that 30 percent of Catholics were thinking about cutting off contributions. These are severe threats to an organization that has the potential to do great things in supporting hospitals, schools, charities, and campaigns against poverty and disease.

The church's slow pace to arrive at an appropriate course of action, and even to acknowledge the incidents, reeks of aristocracy. Church leaders placed themselves upon a pedestal, but popular opinion pulled them down enough to force them to act. To make my opinion clear: it was Evil Barons that created the situation by hiding beneath halos, but it was the Church's aristocracy, its accountability to no one (on earth, anyway), its arrogance, and general incompetence that prolonged it. Each alone is bad enough, but when combined, they are devastating. *It is the chief reason why we must be aware of all the misadventures we face, both in character and in competence, for the wrong combination destroys.*

All organizations must take heed. They need a policy. They need to *continually* train their employees on what constitutes indecency of all sorts. They need to investigate quickly and fairly. They need to act. After all, *action* is an essential trait for knighthood.

A Knight's Code of Business

Decency: A Good Knight strives for decency in the workplace.

And Other Advice

Good Knights, be forever mindful of how your actions may be interpreted, and misinterpreted. Realize that people will think the worst, for it is human nature to do so.

Good Squires-in-Training, ditto to the above. And do not further gossip. It may be entertaining, but those who invite it will someday be the topic of it.

Good Monarchs, tolerate office romances, as they are natural, but quickly draw the line when they interfere with business, for such affairs impact more than you might know. Know, too, that the more decent a kingdom you have, the more likely an Evil Baron will try to hide within it. Beware, and act quickly when you discover one among you, or your slow pace will make matters far more difficult.

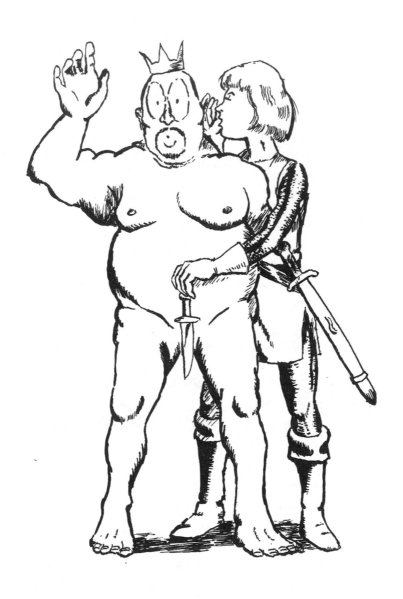

Chapter 6

Anxiety

"In spite of all, Sancho, I beseech you to keep up your courage, for experience will prove to you how great mine is."

—DON QUIXOTE

~

The corporate world can be either a pleasant or a fearful place depending upon the nature of your immediate boss and the tenor set at the very top.

⬧ SURVEY OF 100

Twelve percent agreed (completely or somewhat) that top executives in their companies sometimes use unnecessary fear tactics to keep employees in line. Sixteen percent agreed that they have sometimes felt intimidated about giving their opinions for fear that more-senior executives would not appreciate it.

Courage is vital throughout a kingdom, and throughout a career. It comes in handy when facing Evil Barons who pride themselves on intimidating others, when facing the internal fears we generate ourselves, and even when it becomes necessary to tell a good and kindly Emperor that he has no clothes.

A TALE OF FEAR

Once upon a time many years ago there was a great kingdom that spanned the globe. On one particular day, the nobility of this kingdom was summoned to the great hall for a grand presentation. All the "dents" were there, such as the president, the senior vice presidents, and vice presidents of various kinds. There were nearly 50 in all. Numerous serfs were in the back as well, as handmaidens to the nobility. A buzz of anticipation filled the air as the royal court waited for the event to begin. The buzz fell to silence when the CEO Monarch made an entrance and sat at the head of the great hall, before the royal subjects. The Monarch nodded to me and smiled, acknowledging my presence and beckoning me to begin.

And so I began. I presented the results of a worldwide research study about a key brand owned by this nobility. My aim was to help the nobility set direction, a new course for its most valuable jewel. The research was extensive, and enlivened with a multimedia extravaganza of PowerPoint and videotapes. After delivering important elements of the findings regarding the strength and weaknesses of the brand relative to its competitors, I paused and faced the nobility.

"Given our findings," I said, "there are two plausible strategic paths to take that could catapult this brand to new heights." I then identified each path. But before I recommended which of the two paths I believed showed the most promise, I paused, gazed past the Monarch and directly at the "dents," and invited their opinions before I unveiled my own. I said that I did not want to offer my recommendation first, for fear it would bias the discussion. And so I waited for the nobility to speak, for someone to venture an opinion, to offer a mere thought as to which course of action they believed warranted the most attention.

Silence fell hard within the great hall.

No one dared speak. They were frozen, their eyes all fixed not upon me, but upon the Monarch. Each appeared to be trying to divine what the Monarch's opinion was, as opposed to venturing a guess of his or her own.

The Monarch, on the other hand, was glancing back and forth, from me to the royal subjects, waiting for one of them to venture an opinion. None came. I asked the question again. Again no one, not even the president of the company dared to speak. They were afraid that their answers would, in some way, embarrass them, or worse, contradict what might ultimately be the opinion of the CEO. The risk was too great.

How was this misadventure to end, I remember thinking. I was suddenly conscious that I had made a terrible mistake. I had hoped for the free exchange of ideas, a good debate or two, perhaps even an insight suddenly uncovered through the discourse, but I got none of it, and felt foolish for trying to generate discussion at all.

The Monarch, realizing that the subjects were either too feeble or too afraid to speak, could not bear the silence any longer and spoke, recommending a course of action and rationale that made utter sense. I hit the next slide on my PowerPoint presentation, to reveal that I (the whole company I represented, actually) was recommending the same. We got lucky, I suppose.

What had seemed an inordinate amount of time, was in truth about 30 seconds of uncomfortable silence. Yet, it revealed so much about this particular nobility. They were so afraid of being in disagreement with the Monarch, that they would rather remain silent and risk appearing simple-minded than to venture an opinion and risk being ostracized. This was one of many occurrences of such behavior in this dynasty. The Monarch, either through past behavior or otherwise, created a kingdom of phobics, even at the highest levels within the nobility itself. It was tragic.

Some fall in love with power, and smile inwardly when they know they have inflicted anxiety within the hearts of others. Some use such fear as a weapon of choice. Just take an executive in a public forum and chop off a couple of his or her limbs, and the rest will be kept in line forever.

The fear used by some Monarchs to control the masses typically backfires. For where there is fear, there is also stifled creativity, stagnant innovation, reduced loyalty, greater turnover, decreased productivity and crippled kingdoms. How ironic, that in their desire to control a kingdom, some Monarchs actually lay the groundwork for crippling their realm, assuring that it, and they, will never achieve full potential. Pleasure in instilling fear is a character flaw.

THE IMAGINARY FEAR

However, we must be fair. Some people are intimidated even where there is no intimidation imposed. They just see intimidation everywhere. That is a character flaw, too, one we must all guard against.

Years ago when I worked at Ogilvy & Mather, one of my employees casually mentioned that a couple of the junior account people were afraid to come into my office. I was stunned. The person who told me this thought it was laughable (some of my people often laughed in my face). "How could anybody possibly be afraid of me?" I asked.

Until that day, I always thought I had a wonderful open door policy, one that allowed the free exchange of ideas to flourish in a nonjudgmental environment (Okay. That statement was over the top). I thought I was easy going. What I did not realize was that these junior employees did not always see *me*. Instead, they saw my elevated *title* (I was a senior VP at the time), my corner office, my position on the executive committee, and my direct connection with the highest levels within Ogilvy. They saw the *potential* I had to wield power and influence. It was the potential that I could make their lives miserable that made some of them fear me. It didn't matter that I never shot any one in public (that I remember, at least). It only mattered that *they thought I could*. They were junior, and people more senior were all thought to be wearing broadswords at their waists and lances strapped to their backs, ever ready to strike deep wounds. By the way, there are some people I have known who did this often, so much so, that underlings lived in fear of even those who did not wear broadswords.

From that moment, I realized I had to make extra efforts to overcome a weakness—my own title and the trappings it brought. If I did not, I would never benefit from all the ideas that others could offer. In the great scheme of things, a senior vice president at an advertising agency wasn't all that high up anyway (sorry if I just insulted a ton of people). Imagine what damage people of much higher title can do, without ever realizing it.

It is amazingly common for any given CEO to be in a meeting and make some off the cuff comment, sharing a mild and momentary opinion. Then, the royal court takes over and by the time the serfs hear of the CEO's comment, it has grown into a harsh decree that unless the kingdom does this or that, heads will roll! I have been in countless such situations when employed at an advertising agency where I was told of a client CEO's decree (handed down three levels within the client firm, then over to the advertising agency, and then down another level or two to me). "If we don't do this or that," so said some agency person, "we could lose this business!" Then we wasted an enormous amount of resources to appease the client's CEO who, in fact, *forgot he or she had even made the comment, for it was so trivial at the time.*

Thus, the royal court creates its own fear and bureaucracy fosters it. When I was with General Mills as a young marketing research assistant, in order to communicate with a marketing director, I had to relay a message to my immediate boss who was a research manager, who would discuss it with the research director, who would then stroll down the hall to the marketing director. Now, they were all lovely, bright people, but the formality was a bit intimidating for me, a junior serf.

Those are small misadventures in the grand scheme of things, but when you add a Monarch who loves creating fear, and a kingdom that also manufacturers its own, it is tragic and dysfunctional.

FEAR CAN MAKE US TOO CONSERVATIVE

Fear robs us of our potential. It makes us conservative in a world where adventure is rewarded.

Anonymous Storyteller

When I went to work for Quaker Oats in the mid-1970s, it was a stately and staid old company. Quaker Oatmeal recently had celebrated its 100TH anniversary as a brand, and other big brands— Aunt Jemima, Ken-L-Ration dog food— were well over 50. They still thought of Celeste Pizza as their "new" brand, because it was in the company for "only" about 15 years. Just before I joined the company, a team in R&D came up with yet another way to make a product with oats. (That was the major role of R&D. They used oats in everything from Wolfbrand Chili to chemicals.) Anyway, around the time I arrived on the scene, they had gotten back in-home research on this new product, a mixture of oats and other grains coated with a hardened sugar syrup and extruded into bars. The results were terrific, except management did not take easily to the concept of introducing radically new concepts.

So they had R&D refine the formula a bit and tested it again. Again, it tested with terrific results. The tests and retests went on for the 3+ years I worked there. As I left, the tired, but undaunted brand managers finally pushed management into doing a two-region test market. Six months later, management had to cancel one of the test market regions. Sell through was so strong, the temporary manufacturing facility could not supply both test regions. And so, granola bars were born. The sad thing is that Quaker sat on them for over 3 years after development and testing because of its conservative nature as a company.

▇ SURVEY OF 100

Forty-seven percent agreed (completely or somewhat) that their company asks for new ideas, but doesn't always have the courage to use them.

You just have to love baseball, if only for the metaphors. Hank Aaron is the all time greatest home run hitter, with 755 credited to him. What few realize is that Hank Aaron is also on the list of the top 100 strikeout leaders, with 1383 to his credit. He struck out almost twice as many times as he hit home runs. Moreover, he is not alone. In fact, many home run hitters are on the top strikeout list, including Babe Ruth, Willie Mays, Frank Robinson, Mark McGwire, and Sammy Sosa. You might conclude that because they simply had more at bats, they were apt to make both lists. The true learning is deeper. Their managers overlooked their strikeouts because of their propensity for homeruns. Your success makes people accept your failures. That is the learning. However, many are too afraid to try, so they minimize failures and successes as well. It happens in subtle ways. Some are afraid to make that important presentation, and they are not recognized for their abilities.

Some are afraid to ask for that raise, and hence, they don't get what they are worth. Some are afraid to start their own businesses, and hence, never feel the independence they crave so dearly.

THE SEESAW SYNDROME

The only way to rise up, so some believe, is to push others down. The endless search for criticism instead of praise is one small step toward fostering fear. Yet, it is commonplace. I call this the Seesaw Syndrome (I assume psychologists have some fancy name for it). The following story illustrates the point.

A Story by Paul Kurnit
The Quest for Negativity

   A very sophisticated packaged goods company was caught by the "strength" of its own methodology. Creative meetings were always run in a democratic fashion in which the junior client was expected to provide comments about the advertising first. The goal was to find something bright and inspired to critique about the work. In one session, the work was a no brainer. It was right on in every way. And, the rather sheepish assistant brand manager hesitated and stammered before offering his comment "I'm sorry. I really like it. I can't find anything wrong with it." Following the meeting I feasted upon the group product manager, who admitted that the search for negativity had pre-empted the praise and appreciation for good work.

FEAR MAKES US AVOID TAKING RESPONSIBILITY FOR OUR ACTIONS

Fear of being held accountable, of taking responsibility for poor performance or foul-ups, leads some to point fingers at others. Blaming others absolves people for errors in judgment so that their reputations can stay intact, while hurting the reputation of those they falsely accuse. Fear of taking responsibility for our actions has turned us into a nation that blames others.

   There once was a huge kingdom that was divided into five or so important regions. The kingdom decided to conduct a tracking study to measure brand awareness and perceptions over time. The kingdom asked its advertising agency to design and coordinate the study, and so it did. The coordination wasn't easy, as each of the client's five regions had its own research director. All five directors had their own beliefs as to how the study should be designed. However, after many months of wrangling, the agency finally got all of the regional research directors to agree. The study consisted of a 30-minute telephone survey among a couple of hundred consumers in each region. Each survey would be conducted multiple times in each region in order to track the measures of brand awareness and such over time. Along with the study design, each region's research director approved the sample composition, the questionnaire, and the timing. The study cost nearly a half million dollars.

When the results came in, some of the data from *one* of the five regions looked quirky. To make a long story short, it turned out that this particular region had an abundance of so-called snowbirds—elderly residents who during winter months go to their homes in warmer climates. Their presence in the data appeared to account for the quirks. These snowbirds were not around the rest of the year when the advertising for the brand ran, and therefore, distorted some of the tracking results in that one region.

The client researcher in this region knew of the presence of snowbirds in his territory, but never told the agency that designed the research. They could have been easily eliminated from the study but they were not. The regional folks in that territory decided to blame the agency for "bad data." It is always easier to blame someone else than to accept even some blame. It is a fearful thing to say, "I am partially at fault." It is even more dreadful to say, "I'm totally at fault." Such fear makes many shun responsibility. The research director refused to pay the rest of the research fee (about 50 percent), despite the fact that the quirk affected very little of the information in his region.

It gets better. The remaining four regions, not wanting to be left out, decided they were not going to pay either, despite the fact that the quirk did not affect their regions at all. Now the situation moved to a lack of integrity, all stemming from one regional employee who needed someone to blame, because he was unwilling to take, or even share, responsibility. I suppose he was trying to keep his job, or get a raise, or whatever.

Repeated calls brought no relief, yet the regions continued to benefit from the data for which they were suddenly unwilling to pay. After months of gaining little ground, a miracle happened. The company got new management. The new management began to resolve all outstanding issues. The advertising agency was called in to explain the situation. None of the research directors chose to attend, but instead, sent a representative to make the case for all five regions. Upon hearing both sides of the argument, the new management immediately paid the bill, realizing that the agency designed the study as agreed, based upon the knowledge and input they had been given by the client, and that all of the regional personnel approved everything at every step.

I cannot tell you how refreshing it is to sit at a meeting and hear someone say, "You know, that was my fault. I'll take care of it." Lord knows I have had to make that speech enough times. Alternatively, simply, "I'm part of the blame, I guess I could have . . ." People don't mind if you make mistakes. Make them. Take responsibility. Fix them. Move on. Those who are willing to take responsibility often are praised for their integrity, and those who are always pushing blame elsewhere are often held in lower esteem. Most good military officers know that if something bad occurs on their watch, it is their responsibility. If something wonderful occurs on their watch, they give credit to their people. It is one of the hallmarks of leadership. Fearless leaders take responsibility.

GUTS ARE REWARDED (ULTIMATELY)

I am reminded of two movies. The first is *The Paper Chase*. I first saw this film when I was in college, and it had a deep impact upon me. In the film, our hero Mr. Hart is a first year student at Harvard Law School, and he comes to a realization. He discovers that the students in his Contracts Law class have divided into three behavior types. The first group has given up in the face of the tyrannical professor Kingsfield, and relegated itself to the back of the class, silent, and out of the way of the professor. They fear him greatly. The second group tries, answers Kings-field's questions when called upon, but never volunteers, and never enters the battle. They are fearful, too. The third group, the one to which Mr. Hart aspires, is comprised of those who participate, who raise their hands, and who take a risk and thrust themselves into the fray. "I don't think they are smarter than anyone else," says Mr. Hart, "but they have courage . . . and they will achieve the final recognition." This third echelon runs the risk of grand humiliation, and yet has the chance to receive equally grand rewards. At the end of the film, Hart enters that realm, and is forever changed by it.

The second film is the comedy, *Defending Your Life*. In this film, our hero is an advertising executive who dies and goes to a heavenly plane (called Judgment City) only to discover that he must defend his life in court. The aim of the court is simple: to decide if the person led a life dictated by his fears, or if he faced his fears to become a better human. If he satisfactorily defends his life, demonstrating that he faced his fears when alive, he can move on to the next form of existence. If, however, it is decided that his life was dominated by fears, he will be sent back to Earth and reincarnated, to try again.

These two stories mirror business today. Those who face their fears and participate, who push the limits, even in the face of tyrant kings, are the ones who make it to the top. Yes, they may be fired more often, but that is the risk. Those who do not face their fears are forever huddled in corners, stuck in lower or middle management, taking direction instead of giving it.

I am not the bravest person in the world. Not even close. But most of the fears are under control. In truth, that attitude has been acquired over many years. It also helps that I have had to present to, and confront, dozens of CEOs in my life, and it became all too clear that they are common people with common failings (though some aristocratic CEOs would have us think otherwise). If you are a junior executive, you will eventually learn the same lesson I did, but wouldn't it be grand if you learn it a lot sooner than I did? Face your fears, whatever they may be, and do not be intimidated by those who seek to make you afraid.

Without courage, you cannot battle aristocracies, slay duplicity, unveil larceny, prevent indecency, or right many of the other misadventures you will face. Character traits are often interrelated, and all of them require that you first slay fear.

A Knight's Code of Business

Bravery: A Good Knight must have a brave heart and work to eradicate fear throughout the entire kingdom.

And Other Advice

Good Knights, people will forever follow your lead. Generate no fear in others, confront those that do, and be fearless by example.

Good Squires-in-Training, enter the joust and be impaled a couple thousand times. It doesn't hurt nearly as much as you think it does. If you prove to be fearless, you will have the respect of all. Moreover, if you are fired for your bravery, you will bring that fearlessness with you always.

Good Monarchs, you must work hard to create a kingdom where the subjects do not fear you. Let them follow you because they respect your skills, not because they fear your wrath. Make sure that your idol comments do not become dictates, for your assistants may scurry about creating havoc you did not intend.

Henchmen, Dungeon Keepers and Ogres, feeling fearful much of the time is part of your nature. But hang in there, for while you may fear the Evil Baron or Duchess who employs you, you are more needed by them than you think. They'll protect you.

Evil Monarchs and Barons, you revel in fear. I have no advice for you save this, your company will never achieve its greatest, because the fear you instill to stroke your ego and remain in power is the same fear that will rob you and your company from achieving its full potential.

Chapter 7

Maladies

"I would have your reverence know that I am a knight of La Mancha, by name Don Quixote, and my office and profession is to go through the world redressing injuries and making crooked things straight."

—DON QUIXOTE

Monarchs must be ever vigilant and concerned about many things, and so must Good Knights. The most obvious threats come from beyond the castle walls. Other kingdoms seek to out-compete your own, and other realms even within your kingdom attempt to usurp your power. These keep the royal court quite busy.

Yet some insidious threats come from within the castle walls. These include substance abuse, lunacy, lack of anger control, and more. They are no less damaging to a kingdom than are attacks from foreign lands because they make the subjects within the castle walls weaker, of lower morale, less happy, less productive, and hence unable to defend against outside threats.

A CHARACTER FLAW

Are all of these maladies "character" flaws in the strictest sense? Some will argue not, for there is plenty of evidence to suggest that some such problems arise from physiological sources. However, I will still classify all of them as character flaws for three reasons. First, each affects the way we express our character. Second, each affects the ways others perceive our character. Finally, some employees faced with some of these maladies, such as drug abuse, do not possess enough willpower to stop. Moreover, willpower is an important character trait and a flaw should it be in insufficient quantity.

MALADIES MOST FIERCE

A 2001 study prepared for the Office of National Drug Control Policy found that the cost to society of drug abuse reached $143.4 billion by 1998. It increased an average of 5.9 percent annually from 1992 to 1998. Sixty-nine percent of those costs were in the form of lost productivity. A study in the *Annals of Internal Medicine* found that simple hangovers cost society $148 billion a year in such items as absenteeism and poor job performance. Another study found, "1 in 5 workers report being injured, having to cover for a co-worker, or needing to work harder due to other employees' drinking." Twenty-three percent of American adults suffer from a diagnosed mental disorder, of which 5 to 6 percent are serious. The costs in loss of productivity at work, school, or home were estimated at $78.6 billion as far back as 1990. It is undoubtedly much more than that today.

BusinessWeek reported that on March 25, 2002, the city of St. Cloud, Florida required "applicants for city jobs to swear they've been tobacco-free for a year." Why? Because non-smokers have fewer lost workdays, higher productivity, and lower health insurance costs. In fact, "6 percent to 12 percent of the $1.3 million the city spends on health insurance is tobacco-related," the magazine reported. Smoking is now considered a malady by some, and is perceived to reflect upon not only one's working condition, but *defacto*, upon one's character.

Many incidents caused by character flaws are kept quiet and never make it into the headlines or into the statistics. Many incidents are not even known to those in the next office or floor, and rarely leave the confines of the building.

Anonymous Storyteller

An art director and copywriter at an advertising agency worked side-by-side for many years. Unbeknownst to the copywriter, the art director kept a vial filled with cocaine in his drawer at work, that he would snort routinely. It was years before the partner would discover the truth.

Anonymous Storyteller

A client got blind drunk with his advertising agency buddies. The agency left him at his doorstep at 2:00 a.m. where his family discovered him hours later, asleep.

Anonymous Storyteller

A secretary to a senior VP of sales in a major corporation spent an inordinate amount of time "grooming" in the bathroom. Over time, something bizarre and scary was happening to her face: it was caving in. Turned out that she was a cocaine addict, her nose was collapsing, and she had embezzled over $90,000 from the company to support her habit by creating fake suppliers' invoices.

Incidents that are bigger in proportion make the news. The Associated Press reported an event in which "an ex-employee of a plastics business stabbed two former co-workers and set three others on fire by throwing chemicals at them." Another AP story reported, "America West is firing two pilots charged with trying to fly a jetliner to Phoenix while drunk." The FAA immediately revoked their pilot licenses. One of the two pilots was actually arrested a couple of times before that incident for alleged harassment and domestic assault charges. Character trait and abuse issues have a long history together. Two questions: why weren't these pilots or the madman suspected and caught earlier? Was anybody *really* paying close enough attention?

Many of us are aware of how these maladies are affecting our co-workers to the detriment of their job performance, but many times employees are not aware of what's happening in the next office.

 ## SURVEY OF 100

Twenty-five percent said they are aware of someone in their company whose work productivity is being adversely affected by some sort of malady. These included angry outbursts (20 percent), alcoholism (12 percent), mental disorders (6 percent), or drug abuse (2 percent).

A NOBLE ATTEMPT

Kingdoms have tried to slay these dragons. Many companies offer Employee Assistance Programs (EAP). One survey of human resource professionals found that 67 percent of their organizations offered EAP. Over 66 million workers were enrolled in 2000, which is over twice those enrolled in 1994. Yet, it seems it isn't enough. During this same period, some of these maladies have increased. EAPs do not typically get involved until a problem, as you might imagine, is recognized. Yet it happens that people sometimes prefer not to recognize problems, for it takes emotional resources to deal with them. This is true for both those who have the problem, and for those others in the workplace who are affected by the person with the problem. Still others are not skilled or experienced enough to recognize problems and so they stay hidden for longer than they should.

A PERSONAL RESPONSIBILITY

You work in the kingdom. By that very status, creating a positive environment *is part of your responsibility*. It doesn't matter if you are the highest monarch or the lowest serf. You cannot afford to ignore problems you have when they affect the quality of your work environment. You cannot afford to ignore maladies facing your co-workers when they affect the quality of your work environment. You cannot afford to believe that somehow management will eventually become aware of a particular co-worker's problems and take action to save you from someone who appears unbalanced or alcoholic or whatever. Management may never become aware until it is too late and innocent people could be harmed. Those who are afflicted are sometimes much better able to keep their problems from management than they are from co-workers. They've had practice.

From my experience and observations, *co-workers and underlings, due to proximity to the problem, are often the first line of attack in this battle because they are often the first to know and the first to be affected.* That's a very difficult position for young Serfs, Pages, Squires-in-Training, and even novice Knights to assume. However, it is nonetheless true in many cases. No one is told this in business school, and yet it can affect your life more than you know, for no other reason than your co-worker's problem, if left untreated, may result in personal loss to you; loss in a positive work environment, loss in your morale, loss in your productivity, and, as drastic as it may appear, loss in your own life.

As difficult as it may be at times, each of us is a Knight on a quest to enhance our own workplace. We spend too much time there for it to be otherwise. Unfortunately, that sometimes means that we must address the lack of character in others. This brief chapter is not about maladies in general, or whether your company offers an EAP or not. This chapter is about you, and the way you react to the presence of these afflictions.

Anonymous Storyteller

I was a new division head and I had to hire many new people in a short period. We had a lot of work, but everybody seemed to pitch in well. Then one of my department heads, a new hire that reported directly to me, started acting strange. She began arriving late to work. Her mood would swing from one of excitement to one of melancholy. I asked her what was wrong, and she said that she was having family problems. I felt guilty for prying. So I made allowances for her. Things became better for a time, and then the bad habits resumed. Poor attitude. Tardiness. Absences. Deep melancholy. I was trying to manage a division, yet I was spending a lot of time trying to help my employee better balance what I thought was home and work. However, it was something else. One day, one of her co-workers said he had to tell me something. He looked scared to death. He had seen my new employee taking drugs on the job. Coke. I was floored. I even challenged him, telling him he must be wrong. I guess I felt obligated to defend one of my people, particularly since I just hired her! This was my first time in this situation, and I didn't have any idea what to do. I went to human resources for advice. Then everything moved fast. Our president got involved. Lawyers showed up. Sure enough, it was drugs. It all got resolved, and the woman went into rehab and came out better for it. But it was extremely uncomfortable for a while. I felt stupid that I didn't recognize the signs. I believed what she told me to believe. I'm just glad the co-worker came to me, and we were able to fix the situation before someone got hurt.

A Squire knew he was way over his head, and went to the Knight, who knew he was way over his head, so he went to Human Resources. While management needs to be ever vigilant, the co-workers and underlings are often the first to recognize a problem, and take a brave step toward resolving it. And that's the point.

TEMPER, TEMPER

Business is hectic. People are temperamental, some more than others. As pressure mounts, some people explode in a rush of screams and desk pounding. Some are tyrants all the time. Some are just periodic tyrants. Both can look rather silly. If it cannot be controlled, it is a malady that affects morale and productivity.

A Story by Gary Elliott

Tony was an acknowledged phone-smasher. Tough phone call—cancellations or changes in orders; unrelenting demands from customers; infringements on his time, or news of inhuman deadlines placed upon him produced a physical outburst. First, a deafening barrage of the foulest language—insults strung together with a rhythmic blast and then the beating of his phone. Tony would smash his phone handle on his desk with sledgehammer-like strokes until he broke off the earpiece. He destroyed a phone every two weeks like this. Surrounding employees were at first amused and shocked. His frequency of outbursts made him an outcast. He was counseled and let go sometime later.

Years ago in a galaxy far away, I was sitting in a meeting with a creative director, an account director, and some junior executives. We were discussing a client's business, and the advertising that should be developed. The creative director and account director had an argument most terrible. It started small, and then went big. The account director finally exploded upward sending his chair crashing into the wall behind him, and then marched out of the meeting. The creative director, not wanting to be outperformed, also shot up and dashed off as well. That left me and a couple of junior people sitting in the room.

"Well then," I said, "what are the next steps." We spent the next 10 minutes plotting a course for the advertising, and then arranged a meeting when, hopefully, calmer heads would prevail. I thought nothing more about the event and just went back to work.

Fast forward a couple of years. At a going-away party for one of the junior people, who was now a mid-level manager, I got an unexpected treat. He approached and reminded me of the chair-thrashing event. He said that when it occurred he had been at the agency only a couple of weeks, and that he was ready to quit that day. However, when he saw how I handled the situation, he realized there was hope. So he stayed several more years and left only because he got a job of greater authority and pay.

I was taken aback. I hadn't really thought about my actions until that day. Apparently, my calming influence had made an impact on someone else. I also wondered how many times I had inadvertently showed anger (it happens), and how many people I might have alienated as a result. This junior employee, now a mid-level manager, had a greater impact on me than I had on him. He made me more conscious of my actions, and every time a meeting began to ignite more heat than light, I made a conscious point to try to douse the flames. While I could not prevent people from angry outbursts, I felt a responsibility to fix what I could, where I could. As Don Quixote said, " . . . *making crooked things straight*." Unfortunately, Don Quixote had a habit of making straight things crooked, so practicing what one preaches is important here.

MALADIES ASSASSINATE OUR CHARACTER

Even brief instances of poor judgment hurt. At a going-away party attended by many Knights and the Monarch, a young Squire drank far too much. A Good Knight recognized the signs of impending peril and rushed the Squire out of the restaurant and onto the street corner. As the Knight held the Squire's head, the young Squire tossed a meal and beverages into the street as onlookers passed. It was not a pretty sight. The event did not escape the attention of the royalty. In all other respects, this was a Good Squire with high moral character, but Squires are forever scrutinized for any character flaw. Everything matters. Moments of indiscretion are forever remembered. Demonstrating character is still the coin of the realm. Never, ever think otherwise.

A LITTLE MADNESS IS A GOOD THING

Some Monarchs have been known to be not so crazy as they are eccentric. Sometimes, just sometimes, eccentricity is welcomed. I worked with one particular senior vice president for several years. Soon after I met him, he came to work with a hole in the seat of his pants. His underwear was visible for all to see. I got up a little courage, and I told him so in order to prevent him from being embarrassed further. He smiled and said thank you. He came to work the next week with the same pants, and I told him so again. He smiled and said thank you. By the third and forth time he came to work with the same pants, I realized that he was . . . well . . . eccentric. He went on to become a president of an advertising agency. He was one of the brightest and most enjoyable people I ever knew. A recent genetic study declared that men are more likely to be mutants than are women. In fact, 5.25 times more likely. Since more men are at the CEO level than are women, it might explain a lot.

RELEASE VALVES

While human beings bring afflictions to work, it is also true that the pressures we create at work can heighten the problem. Beyond other duties, I was once put in charge of company morale. It was my duty to organize quarterly events in which the whole office could participate. Bring the families. Bring a date. Let's cut out early on a Friday and blow off some steam. Sometimes we went bowling, sometimes we went to the beach, and sometimes we rented carnival rides at the pier. It was fun, and it allowed people to relax, and toss aside the pressures of business, if only for a day. It did not solve deeply rooted personal problems, but it momentarily lifted a few burdens. For one particular event, I created a carnival atmosphere right in the office. We had carnival games and carnival foods and prizes. Cotton candy was all around. I even rented a fortune-teller to look deep into our employees' auras, and tell them what the future held for them. Things were good. Unfortunately, the fortune-teller could not discern her own fate. The candle she lit to create ambiance was too close to a fire detector in the ceiling. The smoke sounded an alarm, and all floors in our high-rise building were evacuated as several fire trucks rushed to save us. The entire staff went home early. I'm told they liked that, too.

Some people are workaholics (I've been accused of this). That's a malady, too. They stay even after the work is done, and make up more work to do. This not only makes them miserable, but it makes all those around them miserable as well, for many feel they have to compete with the workaholic. Others realize that hours spent does not always equate with productivity.

A Story by Paul Kurnit
Go Home

I was assigned to a very big and prestigious account at the agency. The account supervisor I succeeded was a Harvard MBA— very bright, fastidious and meticulous. He had an oak roll-top desk in his office, which was otherwise decorated accordingly in home study fashion. He lived two blocks from the office. Every night he would go home for an hour, have dinner and come back to the office. Everyone in the group worked every night until at least 11:00 p.m. After all, it was a very important account.

I couldn't believe what I encountered upon taking over the business—hard working people, with no lives and terrible morale. My second week on the job every night at 7:00 p.m. I walked over to people on the account and told them to "go home." I offered no elaboration. The third week I did the same thing but added a comment about something else they might do—have dinner, go to a movie, see friends, work out, watch television, read a book or do nothing—but, "go home" was the continuing mantra. By week four, people started to leave the office as commanded and before 7:00 p.m. By week five, my elixir took hold as the workdays were shorter, productivity improved and morale took a decidedly upbeat turn.

EVIL BARONS?

You will notice that I never called anyone afflicted by these maladies an Evil Baron, and for good reason. Most are not. Most are good people, who have problems that prevent them from achieving their best. There are, however, some I would classify as Evil Barons. That title is reserved for those in senior management who actually encourage some negative behaviors, particularly drinking and carousing. This might include a head of sales, for example, who gets his clients drunk enough to sign a big contract. The title of Evil Baron is also bestowed upon people who pad a contract so that their suppliers can use it to buy them drugs. These are Evil Barons, and can be quite dangerous, too. Beware of them. Only a fully experienced Knight, with the aid of human resources, management, lawyers, and law enforcement can take them on.

A Knight's Code of Business

Well-Being for Others: A Good Knight looks after the personal well-being of those entrusted to him, as well as those who are not, for the kingdom will be better for it.

And Other Advice

Good Knights, your natural inclination to defend your people may actually blind you to truths. Be understanding, but not oblivious.

Good Squires-in-Training, please realize that you are forever watched by those from above. Moments of poor character can last a lifetime. Moreover, if you are afflicted with such maladies as those described herein, never believe, even for a moment, that you can keep them hidden. They will betray you, if you do not slay them first. Though as a co-worker or underling you are often the first line of defense in cases where the afflictions of fellow employees are creating a poor work environment, you must be careful and use good sense. Seek the aid of those within your company who have experience in such matters, typically human resources. Helping others resolve personal maladies is best left to the experts.

Good Monarchs, realize that the pressures you level upon employees can serve to exaggerate human maladies. Create a lighthearted atmosphere to lessen the pressures that arise from time to time. It will not fix all the world's problems, but it will lessen some ills within your corner.

Evil Monarchs & Barons, your tendency to engage in and encourage bad behaviors will defeat you, for it makes you and your employees weak.

Chapter 8

Insincerity

"He must be chaste in thought, a man of his word, generous in action, valiant in deed, patient in adversity, charitable to the needy, and finally, a maintainer of the truth, although its defense may cost him his life."

—Don Quixote

∽

This chapter begins with a tale of two kingdoms and two presentations. They serve to illustrate the faces we sometimes hide behind, thus to mask our true feelings.

In the late 1980s in Los Angeles, Ogilvy & Mather Advertising assembled a dedicated team to pitch two important pieces of new business. Both were to rather large and noteworthy kingdoms. The first was Microsoft and the second was Paramount Pictures. The presentations were scheduled about a day a part, so panic ensued as the new business team at Ogilvy & Mather raced and worked and slaved to understand both companies and their industries in a very short time.

New business in an advertising agency is always an adventure, because by industry convention, an advertising agency cannot pitch business if it already has a client in that industry, due to supposed conflict of interests (even in offices a world apart). Hence, an agency probably cannot pitch Ford in Europe if it already has General Motors in South America. Here's the catch. If an agency can pitch only business in new industries, it means that the agency lacks current experience in

that arena. Hence, agencies are always pitching business from a position of initial incompetence, and then must work like crazy over a very
short time to gain knowledge and insights that it has taken others
decades to obtain. Incompetence to competence in a short time is the
nature of every single new business effort. There may be members of
the new business team that have prior experience, and though useful,
it is often dated, like a can of sardines left open on a patio through a
hot summer.

After several weeks of arduous labor, research, a slew of helpful and
not so helpful advice from people around the world, the time was upon
us to pitch each piece of business. We were ready, and we had an edge.
Our new business leader was Gary Elliott, who was without a doubt
one of the best leaders (Knights) I ever had the good fortune to follow.
Intricate presentations were assembled, detailing how each of these
wonderful brands could be taken to new heights, by people who had,
until several weeks earlier, little knowledge about either organization. I
needed to explain the process to you, to give you greater appreciation
for what transpired afterwards.

INSINCERITY UNMASKED

Day One was the Microsoft pitch. Over a dozen Microsoft corporate
communication executives filled the room at Ogilvy, sitting around a
U-shaped table, with the presenters entering the U to speak to the
guests. The presentation took the form that most new business pitches
take, beginning with brief introductions, then a reason why we were all
gathered, then a launch into a strategic framework that included the
issues facing the brand, the opportunities, the recommended strategy,
followed by the creative approach to bring the strategy to life, and then
the media plan. During earlier rehearsals, the Microsoft presentation
came to about an hour and thirty minutes uninterrupted. We assumed
that, with questions from the client, the presentation would run a full
two hours. Max.

But that was not to be. The meeting lasted nearly five grueling,
exhausting, mind-bending hours. It was described by some afterwards
as "brutal." Each member of the presentation team was blasted with

dozens of questions, challenging every assumption, baiting us with alternative options to see if we had considered different solutions, drilling deeper and deeper into our reasoning, and into every comment. I was responsible for delivering the strategic portion of the plan, and was therefore one of the first members of the team to feel the burst. It was far more intense than any pitch I had given prior or since. When I finally passed the presentation over to the creative director, I was a bit unnerved, never having been so attacked by so many, with exacting questions that flew without pause. I sat slowly back into my chair, next to the then chairman of Ogilvy, Graham Phillips. He passed a note to me stating, "Well done!" I thought he was crazy, unless of course, he meant "well done" like a barbecued steak.

So it went, through creative and through media. Microsoft challenged everything, leaving us with the belief that we had clearly missed the bull's-eye. At last the meeting came to a long overdue end, and all the presenters crawled out of the presentation room and retreated to our offices for a short respite. We realized we had lost, and had, for some reason, completely misread what Microsoft needed, and in so doing, tried to sell Microsoft a point of view they were clearly not buying.

But this was advertising where misadventures abound. Besides, we'd only had a couple of weeks or so to understand their business. Oh well. Next!

We shook off the disappointment and launched ourselves into the Paramount pitch the next day (I took a minor role). What a sweet difference in the reception. Every recommendation the team made, the client seemed to buy, and greeted it with smiles and nods. The chemistry was ideal. The conference room was even decorated to resemble a theater, complete with a marquee and a popcorn stand. If there was ever a perfect match, this was it. The team left the meeting feeling rather good. We were redeemed from the previous day's ordeal. "At least we won Paramount," we mused. Good job!

Within a week, we were stunned to learn that we had won Microsoft. Won! It was the most significant win for the Los Angeles office of Ogilvy & Mather ever. Just as shocking, we had lost the Paramount pitch. Lost!

How could we have misread the signs? There was learning in all of this. Understanding corporate culture is everything, especially when judging sincerity. The same goes for people.

Microsoft's culture was about criticism, and using it to find unadulterated truth. They knew we'd had only a couple of weeks to understand their business, and they were determined to find out if we were faking it. Their tactics focused upon examining our knowledge to see how deep it ran, to see if we had considered alternatives, to understand the depth of our intellect, and to see if we buckled under the pressure of scrutiny. They, in essence, were bent upon stripping us of our veils, to see if we were made of substance, or alternatively, whether we were made of nothing at all. The Microsoft executives, as it turned out, were the same people on the inside that you saw on the outside. They were straightforward in their approach, though sometimes brutally indelicate in their methods. They were driven, intellectual, a tad arrogant, and in relentless pursuit to discover if the person before them was another intellect or a charlatan. If they thought we missed an important point, they jabbed it in our face. If they thought we missed a small point, they jabbed it in our face. When we made our case, they stopped the barrage, but we never heard any praise for our efforts during the presentation, despite the fact that they apparently liked much of what they heard.

Paramount lived in a different culture, one of pleasantries, hugs, and praise, which often served to hide criticism. Such a culture is fraught with good manners and pleasant appearances, but it masks the truth about how people really feel. We mistook their approach. We thought the friendly nods and gestures meant they agreed with us. It only meant they were being pleasant with us. They were insincere, though many can argue that they simply had better manners.

The Microsoft vs. Paramount example, though extreme, provides some interesting learning. The first gave us little praise, just criticism. The second gave us little criticism, just praise. I don't know if these companies are the same today as they were then. However, at that moment in time, neither was being completely sincere. Microsoft was insincere by withholding praise for what turned out to be a welcomed presentation, and Paramount was insincere by withholding criticism, for apparently we fell short relative to what another agency had to offer.

Eventually, Ogilvy did win Paramount on the next try one year later. However, during that second pitch we were more aware that appearances do not tell you what is really on a person's mind. We were wiser. We also became wiser when we were more exposed to Microsoft's culture, for we did not always mistake criticism for failure. This became especially handy when we eventually had to present our advertising plans to Bill Gates.

INFECTED WITH INSINCERITY

The corporate world is infected with insincerity, providing either too much unwarranted praise or too much unwarranted criticism. This is a character flaw. We hide our true feelings because we do not want a confrontation, or we don't want to hurt someone's feelings, or we think that such confrontations are simply bad manners, or we are being devious, or we enjoy being more critical than need be. However, this attitude prevents us from telling companies and individuals the truth about their performance, and that gets in the way of us achieving our best.

 SURVEY OF 100

Twenty-two percent agreed (completely or somewhat) that their top executives are often insincere with employees on corporate or personnel matters; 27 percent agreed that they themselves sometimes have difficulty telling a subordinate or co-worker the truth about his or her job performance.

It happens at all levels, and in many situations. Some managers give favorable evaluations to employees because they cannot bear to look into their eyes and tell them the harsh, and even not so harsh, truth. When managers aren't truthful with employees, they simply continue to do what they were doing, lowering the productivity of departments or even the company as a whole without even realizing that their performance is sub par. Other managers have difficulty dispensing praise, though are ever quick to criticize. This destroys self-esteem. Some managers avoid providing evaluations altogether. They always seem to be too busy. This creates confusion and uncertainty. Yet, I have seen others who always find the time no matter how busy they are, because they know the impact that sincere appraisals can have on an employee, a department, and the kingdom as a whole.

When we avoid sincerity, when we cannot tell our employees the truth about their performance (good and bad), we are doing a disservice to them and to the company.

CHEESE ON YOUR TIE

This is a silly story. However, I think it demonstrates a point. When I was an employee at General Mills, I was often in the test kitchens to try new products scheduled for research. One morning I tasted a new formula for a noodle dish, and then I ran to other meetings throughout the day, encountering dozens of people. When I got home that evening, I discovered that a big glob of bright orange cheese had fallen on my dark blue tie from that morning. I was amazed that I had not noticed it, and more amazed that not a soul in all the other meetings I had attended during the rest of the day had said anything. The next day I asked several colleagues whether they had noticed the cheese on my tie the day before. They each smiled a bit sheepishly, and said, "Yes." I asked them why they didn't say anything. They each said, "Because I didn't want to embarrass you." I responded with, "So . . . what you did then was to send me off to embarrass myself in front of others for the rest of the day!" They fell silent.

Employees deserve to be told the truth. If they are not, how can they rise to the level that is expected of them? Metaphorically, they have cheese on their ties for all to see, but if they don't know it, they can't take it off, and they should not be held accountable for it. I have been in countless meetings about personnel, and have been amazed at the number of employees that would complain about a colleague. When I asked if they told the colleague of their complaint, they inevitably said "No." I would send them off to tell the colleague directly. You should not complain about the failings of colleagues if you are not prepared to face them directly. That's like leaving cheese on their tie, then pointing it out to others, without giving them the chance to fix it. It is not easy to always fix it, for some people like cheese on their ties, and others will claim there is no cheese, but at least you tried.

INSINCERITY COSTS

A former colleague (notice I said "former") called me a couple of years ago in need of help. Let's call him John. He owned a small advertising agency, and I had started my own consulting practice. John asked that I spend a day working with him and one of his clients to generate directions for the client's brands. While most of my clients are global in nature, and occupy most of my waking hours, I decided to help John because we had worked together for several years at another company. I told John that my fee would be $1,000 for the day, and John agreed. This was less than I charge other clients, because I wanted to do a favor for John and because his agency was small. In actuality, I spent two days on the assignment. I allocated a full day before the client session to generate ideas on my own, so that I would be sure to make my colleague look good in front of his client. I also spent about $200 on products to bring to the session to help the client think outside the box. This is peanuts, I know, but this story needed a little context.

The client session went extremely well, judging by the client's comments afterward. As a parting gift, I gave John's clients a marketing book that I had previously written. John's clients thanked me profusely, as did John. Afterwards, John took me aside and talked about other ways I could help. It was a pleasant experience all around.

However, John never paid me the $1,000. I called after a month, and John said the check was in processing. After three months, I called again. He didn't return my call, or the one I placed after that. I was suddenly more worried about his business than my $1,000—a small sum in the grand scheme of things—and told him so in the voice messages. I asked him if I could help in any way. I never heard back from him, though associates we have in common told me that he continues to run the agency and pitch new business.

One might conclude that he is an Evil Baron. I don't actually think so (okay, maybe he is). I prefer to think that either he was on the verge of bankruptcy and didn't have $1,000, or that I did a terrible job with his client, and he could not face telling me. I kept an open mind, and realized it could go either way. If I did a terrible job, I would have gladly excused the money and made amends. If he was near bankruptcy, I would have traded the $1,000 for a shot at another project down the road when his company was more solvent. These kinds of things can be fixed, if only people are sincere with one another.

Six months after this incident, a couple of different people asked me what advertising agencies I would recommend for their business. I gave them the name of an agency, *but I could not give them John's.* Caught between helping a colleague who appeared to be insincere at the very least, and people who trusted me to provide them with agency names that could help them, I had no choice. I felt bad about it, but I could not be sure that John would be sincere in his dealings with these other people. John potentially lost many thousands of dollars in new work because, for some reason, he could not level with me.

Here's another story. Some people lavish too much praise on some, and damn others for reasons that appear suspect. When they do, all of their praise becomes suspect, and they damage their own reputations.

Anonymous Storyteller

At a company I worked for, the beginning of every month started with a company meeting to talk about results, give birthday well wishes, etc. At these meetings, the owner of the company always loved to talk about how he considered us his family. While this sounds great in theory, when any employee left the company to go to a different company, the owner would take a moment in the company meeting to let you know his feelings about the employee who left. Because these employees left "the family," the owner usually talked about them as if they were traitors and said they wouldn't be missed. For those of us who remained and had worked with these people and had come to know and respect them, it didn't exactly make us feel good about being in the owner's "family"—especially since we knew we'd be bad mouthed once we left. Over time many people left because of the hostility displayed by the owner in these monthly "family" gatherings.

Praise should be given when deserved, and withheld when not deserved. The same applies when offering criticism. In the great majority of cases, a little praise and a little criticism are what most of us need and deserve.

A Knight's Code of Business

Sincerity: A Good Knight will be sincere with all people, in ways that are direct though respectful, balancing the appropriate degree of praise and criticism.

And Other Advice

Good Knights, start with praise, then with helpful criticism. The former allows the latter to be more easily digested. Combined, they often equal sincerity.

Good Squires-in-Training, if your boss only criticizes and dispenses little praise, chances are you are either truly not suited to your current job, or he's simply an Evil Baron who, as we discussed in a previous chapter, feels that he rises in stature when he lowers others (seesaw syndrome). In any case, you must seek a new boss, a new kingdom, or a new vocation.

Good Monarchs, be forthright with your employees, customers and clients. They appreciate sincerity more than you will know.

Evil Monarchs & Barons, your insincerity will cost you more in the end through lost business and fleeing employees. In addition, this chapter does not give you the license to brutalize your people under the banner of "sincerity."

This chapter concludes our exploration of the essential issues of character, though we will revisit character issues even in the following section that pertains to competence.

At this stage in the book, you would be right to ask how we can achieve high moral character in an intense, fast-paced business world where often there is little time to think about our character when a multitude of decisions and compromises have to be made quickly. In his book, *Defining Moments*, author Joseph L. Badaracco, Jr. offers counsel, derived from teachings of the Roman emperor and philosopher, Marcus Aurelius. First, you owe it to yourself, and should work hard, to "create moments of serenity" where you can "slow down and step back, to withdraw and reflect." Second, you should use those moments "as a preparation for the tasks of everyday life and work," by learning what you can from your past experiences and the experiences of those around you. Finally, the author shows that Marcus Aurelius "understood the value of looking up from the urgent tasks of the moment and placing them in the larger context of the life he wanted to live." Are your smallest decisions and actions at work contributing to the larger virtues you admire? That's a question we need to always ask ourselves as we strive to attain high moral character.

In their book, *The Power of Ethical Management*, authors Norman Vincent Peale and Kenneth Blanchard offer this simple Ethics Check based upon three questions. Is your intended action legal? Is it balanced (fair to all concerned)? In addition, how does it make you feel about yourself?

That is something to think about. Now we turn our attention to matters of competence . . .

Misadventures
in Competence

~

Introduction to Competence

Competency is the condition of being fit to do one's job. Increasing competency is simply the movement towards greater and greater levels of performance. Incompetence is the opposite. Some people never perform their current job at what might be considered an adequate level of competence. Those who do attain competence in a specific job often don't realize that the skills needed to perform that job may change over time, and so they must change with it so as to *stay* competent. Importantly, competence is not just about tangible things such as technical expertise. It is more about intangible things, such as passion and vision. It is these attributes that drive our ability to attain greatness.

SURVEY OF 100

On average, our research found that 84 percent of employees are believed to be fully competent in their current position. That leaves 16 percent that are not. We also found that 74 percent are believed to consistently strive to increase their competence, whereas 26 percent do not.

With roughly one-sixth of a company's employees believed to be incompetent, and a quarter who are not trying to increase their competence, misadventures are sure to happen even at the highest levels. At its worse, incompetence will destroy kingdoms and bring down the nobles from their high perches. In its mildest form, incompetence will insure that kingdoms never achieve what they desire, either as a whole or as individuals.

The chapters in this section are about the subtle, and not so subtle, forms of incompetence. Those who have high moral character yet low competence are truly the namesakes of Don Quixote. Yet all they need to do is to ignite the passion for greater competence, slay their delusions, and many good things will follow. Those who have low competence and low character are dangerous foes, as discussed earlier, particularly if they eventually find their way into middle and upper management, for they will ruin their companies to serve selfish ends.

To whet our appetite for incompetence, we asked our Survey of 100 to compete this sentence: "The most incompetent thing I ever saw in my company was when . . ."

Here are some of the responses:

"Someone was promoted who was not qualified. His peers knew he was not qualified, but he got promoted anyway."

"They gave control of the company to a new CEO and president who everyone knew was obviously not the right person for the position."

"They launched a product that clearly wasn't ready."

"One of the HR people doesn't know how to use Microsoft Office. This is very incompetent in 2002."

"We sued (client's name) in an effort to get the proposal approved. You do not sue the people who you need to approve the proposal. The suit was dropped, but bridges were burned."

"We sold a division off and had to reacquire it at twice the cost."

"We failed to purchase a competitor who was in bankruptcy. The purchase would have increased our market share from fifty to seventy percent."

"Our president got rid of most of his direct reports by making it uncomfortable for them to stay, rather than dismiss them. The problem was it took a long time and a lot of effort."

"The sales force didn't follow up on an obvious opportunity in the marketplace."

"When top management refused to accept new technology, particularly the advent of the Internet."

"An executive tried to settle a trademark dispute entirely without any guidance from anyone dealing in that area. This was a dispute outside the executive's area."

"We decided to add a new service and didn't run a cost benefit analysis."

"We hired people who didn't have experience for the job."

"We laid off a qualified worker at the whim of the supervisor."

"Carelessness on the production; there are steps on how to assemble and they're trained to follow them. A worker missed or skipped some steps even when the proper instructions were in front of him and a customer received a product that didn't work."

"Employees leave and then they have exit interviews and bring up things that should have been settled before."

We will now discuss the roots of incompetence, so that we might learn from the follies and misadventures of others, thus avoiding similar fates. The chapters and topics we will discuss in this section include deficiencies in passion, lack of a visionary or vision, scarcity of good communication, mediocrity, tomfoolery (style overwhelming substance), and futility.

Chapter 9

Passion Deficiency

"Knights-errant, Sancho, knew, and ought to know, somewhat of all things, for there have been knights-errant in past ages who were as ready to make a sermon or a speech on the king's highway as though they had taken their degrees at the University of Paris; whence it may be inferred that the lance never blunted the pen, nor the pen the lance."

—DON QUIXOTE

Passion for your trade is the cornerstone of competence. If you are not passionate, everything else will suffer. You will neglect training and you will neglect details. The natural state of some human beings appears to be as follows: learn enough to get by, and then stop learning. This may be due to laziness or lack of talent, but from my observations, it is typically due to a woeful lack of passion.

 SURVEY OF 100

Thirty-seven percent completely agreed that employees in their companies are truly passionate about their chosen profession; 51 percent agreed only somewhat, suggesting that many people are not as passionate as they could be. Eleven percent disagreed that people in their companies are passionate about their chosen profession; 1 percent did not know or refused to answer.

People who truly care about their craft will take the time to learn all things related to it. They are the ones who will often rise to the top because they care about learning how to do things right. They also want to learn how to avoid the mistakes made by others. They are forever students. Some among those go one step further by breaking new ground and making a true contribution to knowledge in their chosen field. "I'm not an educator, but I am a learner," said Bill Gates in his book *The Road Ahead.* "And one of the things I love best about my job is that I'm surrounded by other people who love to learn."

Passion inspired Don Quixote to read all there was to learn about knights. Passion made him rush off to his adventures. Unfortunately, it was a lack of good judgment and a plethora of delusions that made him fail. However, this chapter will focus upon passion, the starting place of competence. It will also show how lack of passion and its related misadventures can come between us and achieving our best.

PASSION FOR UPWARD LEARNING

I had the good fortune to begin my career at General Mills in market research. At that time, the new hires did not enter any division for a couple of months. Instead, we went into a training program until we mastered enough skills to be allowed to touch one of the company's brands. I hated the training at the time, for having just completed my MBA, I thought I had all the skills necessary to begin making a real impact. I thought I knew all I needed to know. I was completely, utterly wrong. The training program proved invaluable, and I learned a great deal about my chosen profession. Only then was I truly competent to be a new hire. I was forever grateful.

That early experience taught that each of us needs a passion for *continued, upward learning.* We must be students of our craft, and assume that we do not know it all. Once you think you have all the answers, you stop looking for more questions. *It's best that you always assume you are incompetent, for that attitude will help you remain competent.* Assuming you are incompetent is the only way you will kick yourself in the backside in order to investigate new approaches and learn new skills and be competent in new jobs. Passion for upward learning is essential.

However, human nature, organizations, and circumstances keep intervening.

Once upon a time in an advertising kingdom, an associate creative director was hailed as great and he *was* extremely talented in his vocation. On that, there is no argument. So great was he, that he was stolen by a nearby kingdom and installed as the new creative director to run an entire creative department of many dozens. The reasoning? He was magnificent in his current task as an associate creative director, and so he was ready for the next step—to be a beacon of encouragement and inspiration to the new armies he would now command.

It was disastrous. He managed to deflate the talented staff he was there to lead, ignoring the fine work the agency had done to date. He did not encourage. He criticized with the arrogance of an entitled crowned prince, not the delicate encouragement of a seasoned statesman. Many talented people exited. The creative director's actions also suggested that he believed that his job was the same as it had always been, to be an associate director. So, as the staff of very talented creative professionals huddled in their offices, waiting for assignments to prove their worth, the new creative director gave them few, hoarding much of the work for himself, instead of leading and teaching others.

He was incompetent to have his new job, and he did not know it. He had no formal training in leadership, or so it appeared. However, this was a dual failure. First, on the part of the agency that brought him in, thinking that past skills at a lower job equate to a much loftier job requiring a whole different skill set. Second, it was a failure of the creative director himself, for not realizing fast enough that his job had changed, and that he had to rise to a whole new set of competencies. He had no passion to learn a new set of skills, because he felt comfortable in the old ones. The creative director left within a short time. He remains talented, to be sure. Perhaps, along the way, he eventually learned to lead and to inspire. A new creative director who knew what it meant to hold the title re-built and re-energized the department at great effort.

ARE WE PASSIONATE ENOUGH?

It is one thing to say we are passionate, but quite another to prove it with our actions. As one small indicator of how committed professionals are, we asked our Survey of 100 marketers if they had read trade magazines, marketing newsletters, or a marketing book in the past year. The percentages who said yes were 96 percent, 94 percent, and 73 percent respectively. Not bad. We also asked if they *ever* read notable marketing books including a couple marketing classics and a couple contemporary best sellers. Here are the books and the percentage of marketers who claim to have read each:

Any marketing book by Philip Kotler: 32 percent,

Ogilvy On Advertising by David Ogilvy: 27 percent,

The 22 Immutable Laws of Marketing by Ries and Trout: 21 percent,

Positioning, The Battle for Your Mind also by Ries and Trout: 20 percent,

Why We Buy by Paco Underhill: 16 percent,

The Tipping Point by Malcolm Gladwell: 4 percent, and

None of the above: 42 percent!

Of course, there are other marketing books they could have read, but some of those cited above are considered "must reads" for all marketers. My point simply was to demonstrate that there is a range of passion. Many say they have passion, but fewer actually follow through to gain the fundamentals they need. Here is an indication of that range of passion: 58 percent of those surveyed read at least one of these books, 39 percent read two or more, 16 percent read three or more. Zero percent read all of them. My guess: those who read the most are the ones who will most likely be the standouts. While this survey focused upon marketing executives, I am willing to bet that these same findings would parallel other disciplines as well.

Those who ignore the teachings of others always surprise me. They prefer to learn everything on the job by trial and error, oblivious to the wisdom that others have spent a lifetime to obtain. When I was at Ogilvy & Mather, for example, I was amazed at *some* in the creative department who paid little heed to *Ogilvy On Advertising*. They said they felt "confined" by what they perceived as rules David had created.

Yet, many of those who felt confined *never actually read the book* (thumbing through the pages at warp speed does not count as reading). That is insanity, and arrogance, and a waste of resources when companies have to continually train people because of their tendency to ignore the wisdom of others. It is okay to break and advance the rules of those who came before, as long as you took the time to learn them beforehand.

I was often asked to interview all potential key hires in the Los Angeles office of Ogilvy. My interview questions were designed to understand if the people sitting before me were students of the advertising craft. Were they passionate? One simple question was this: "Tell me what current advertising you admire and why, and then tell me which advertising you hate and why?" That simple question would trip up half of the interviewees, even very senior ones. I did not actually care what advertising they liked and disliked. I just wanted to see whether they had actually thought about the question, the speed at which the answers came to them, the arguments they made. That told me if they had passion, and if they were students of their craft.

One last point here, for the record: I must admit that I continually have to kick myself in the backside. Learning new stuff doesn't come naturally. However, I am grateful for a host of clients and colleagues who push me, as I do them on occasion. That helps a lot.

FOSTERING THE WRONG KIND OF PASSION

Some organizations and circumstances foster the wrong kind of passion. Aristocracies, for example, can foster a great passion to obtain entitlements, dwarfing the passion to learn the craft of management. At the very least, it is another terrible waste of resources; at the most, it's quite dangerous.

Ralph was a loyal guy—a very loyal guy. He was so loyal to the Monarch he worked for that the King decided to bestow upon Ralph the exalted title of marketing director. That was a good title for one who was, until that day, not in marketing, and had no formal training in marketing whatsoever. None. Zip. Nada. However, the Monarch cared little for that, for Ralph had been loyal for many years, and Ralph coveted a role as marketing director. *His passion was in coveting the title, not in learning and extending the discipline.* So Ralph vacated his office in some little-known department and, in a very brief time, was whisked into meetings on marketing strategy, new advertising campaigns, and in-store point-of-sale materials.

The people around Ralph held his hand in an attempt to bring him along, teach him the basics, and ensure that he did not do anything to destroy the brands he now managed. In fairness to Ralph, he learned little by little over time, due to the efforts of all concerned. The trouble was he didn't learn much more than was necessary. Ralph spent a lot of his time on the golf course with various vendors who wanted his business, one of the perks of marketing. Ralph's inexperience and the resources expended by those around Ralph to help him do his job did not help the brand achieve its best. It actually slowed things down. He was not a bad guy. But it was not the best idea to put him where he was. Such incidents also created disappointment among others in the organization that had the training and the passion for the job, but not the chairman's ear.

Do you know a Ralph or someone like him?

Ralph was incompetent to have his job. He did not have the passion for the job, but only for the things the job offered: the pay, the title, the authority, and the rewards. However, the Monarch did not see that, nor did he seem to care. After all, this was about bestowing favors, not about merit. The truth is that "Ralph" is not one person, but a composite of several people I have seen over the years who found themselves in a position for all the wrong reasons.

Fortunately, most Ralphs don't mistakenly destroy their companies, but some high profile ones have, demonstrating that the *wrong kind of passion* can be quite damaging. High-profile cases such as Enron may reveal in time that a combination of self-interested aristocrats, and their intense passion for wealth and achievement, overwhelmed the passion for sound management practices, leading to the downfall. One executive told me that, "The people I met at Enron, and there were several, were passionate about their craft; their spirit of invention, and their entrepreneurship. They loved the optimism and promise of Enron.

Money was important; but empowerment to achieve was dominant."

Some are so intent upon success, and fostering success, that they are unwilling to hear facts to the contrary. Passion for success can blind them if they are not careful.

Anonymous Storyteller
Refusing to hear the facts.

I was working on a video game business during the boom of the early 1980s, when sales of video game systems like Atari, Intellivision and Colecovision were rocketing skywards. We were also about to launch a low cost home computer, supposedly the next big product craze.

As a newcomer to the group, I was given all the data we had in the fall of 1982 (sales trends and projections, consumer research, trade studies etc.) and asked to develop a marketing and communications recommendation for 1983. I analyzed the data and concluded that sales of video game hardware would decline by 5 percent in 1983, and that low-cost home computers would sell about 3.5 million units (half what was then being forecast in the press).

My boss told me we couldn't possibly present those figures to the client. No one would believe them. They were ridiculous. The market was booming! I must have made a mistake, and had to find some "rational" way to massage my figures upward into a more acceptable range. I did as I was told.

In 1983, sales of video game hardware went down about 5 percent, low-cost home computers sold about half what had been projected, the bottom fell out of the market and our client almost went bankrupt. They lost more in one year than they had gained on the whole video game business in the previous three years because no one wanted to hear the real facts.

MATCHING TALENTS TO JOBS IGNITES PASSION

All people have some natural talent. Most of us never figure out what our talent is, but for those that do, matching the right talent to the right job is explosive. Matching talents with jobs is a critical step toward achieving competence as an organization.

There once was an assistant named Ben who got a job in an advertising agency in the research and planning department. His job was to do what assistants do, which was to assist a senior vice president (me) in his daily duties. That meant typing letters, filing, coordinating meetings, and such. Ben was also the assistant to the entire department, and performed these same duties for others as well.

Ben was not suited for this task. He was, in fact, the worst person ever put into this role. Memos were not completed on time, filing was not done, meeting screw-ups happened with regularity. The department screamed to the senior vice president, "Let's get rid of this guy!"

"In time," said the SVP.

"Why not now?" complained the staff.

"Because," said the SVP. "While Ben is a terrible assistant, his background and abilities in creative pursuits tells me he should be in the creative department as a copywriter. I need to buy time, to find Ben an assistant's position in the other group so that his talents can be put to better use." A short time later, a position did open and Ben was transferred. He became a copywriter, then an associate creative director, and then a creative director.

Someone once told me that there are no incompetent employees, just employees in the wrong jobs. It is incumbent upon Good Knights to find the talents in their employees and use them where they best fit. However, it is also incumbent upon employees to recognize where their talents, interests, and passions lay.

A Story by Mark Rice

I worked in Hong Kong for a couple of years back in the 1980s. I was media director, and wanted to expand my wings a bit. The head of the office gave me the title of account director on Parker Pen. On my first day in the new role, the creative director on the business had just completed a new ad, and told me to go sell it to the client. It was a Christmas ad, with hand-written sheet music. It was beautifully laid out, and laid across the top of the ad was the new roller ball Parker Pen. The title of the hand written sheet music was "Jingle Balls."

I went to the client, by myself, to "sell" the ad that day; no strategy, no set up, just the ad. This was my first day as an account *person so I wanted everything to go well. I showed the client the ad, saying something quite brilliant, along the lines of "Here it is." The client, who was Asian, said, "I don't get it."*

I replied that the creative director was confident it would be quite clear to consumers in Asian markets. The client asked if I had alternatives, and I replied that the creative director very much liked this ad, and did not see the need for an alternate. The client asked if I thought it would be an effective ad and I said probably not. When asked why I was presenting an ad I did not believe in, I told him that if an experienced creative director liked the ad, who was I to say something negative. I was politely sent back to the office and asked to look at other ideas.

I went back and told the CD the client would like something else. I also said that I had zero interest in being an account person anymore if it meant selling clients ads that I did not like.

Good move.

The authors of the book *First, Break All the Rules* surveyed some 80,000 managers to discover what the world's greatest managers do differently. One observation: "As a manager your job is not to teach people talent. Your job is to help them earn the accolade 'talented' by matching their talent to the role."

PASSION FOR DETAILS

I hate details. We all hate details. As it happens, taking care of the details allows the big things we love to go well. Details are alive, and their aim is to screw us up and make us look bad. They will do just that unless we corral them (I know this from experience). Here are a couple of stories about everyday incidents that aim to defeat us. They all have one thing in common, an important detail gone amuck.

Anonymous Storyteller

Once upon a time, a business unit in a large consumer packaged goods company was initiating Spanish-language advertising to the U.S. Hispanic market. As all good brand managers do, they asked the research department to set up and execute an awareness and usage tracking study to help measure the effects of the advertising campaign. The research department was all too happy to comply, and because of limited marketing budgets, set up a wave-to-wave survey.

The first interviewing wave (pre-wave) was completed just before the advertising campaign launched. Results were shared with marketing, establishing a base level of awareness. Everybody was happy, and all looked forward to the campaign's anticipated positive results!

Five months later, after the advertising campaign went off-air, the post-advertising consumer survey was conducted. Results were reported, and to everybody's shock and disappointment, the data showed that not only had all key measures not improved, they had actually dropped. Awareness, purchase intent, imagery—all below the pre-advertising flight levels.

"It can't be!" they shouted.

"Impossible!" they insisted.

And most of all, they relied on the age-old marketing excuse, crying, "The data must be wrong! The research is bad!"

The research department contacted the research vendor, imploring, "The data must be wrong!" But the research vendor responded that no, the research was valid.

Therefore, the team went back to work looking for an explanation. After considering all possibilities over several days, they concluded: "The data must be wrong!"

The research department again contacted the research vendor, again insisting that the data must be flawed. But the research vendor, now sweating, reiterated that after checking, the research was valid.

Perplexed, nobody knew what to make of the results, other than to possibly blame the advertising agency for ineffective creative.

Then one day a couple of weeks later, in a meeting completely unrelated to the new Hispanic advertising, one of the associate brand managers was proudly showing a tape of the new Spanish-language ad to a representative of a large Hispanic TV network.

"We ran this commercial on your network for about five months," the associate proudly declared.

"It's a nice commercial," responded the network representative,

"But I don't remember ever seeing it at the station."

Both of them confused, the network representative went back to the network, checked into it, and later contacted the associate, confirming that the ad had never run on his network.

Or, as it was quickly discovered, on any network at all, thanks to a contract employee at the ad agency who, after extensive media planning, forgot to actually purchase the television airtime.

And another:

Anonymous Storyteller
Getting your timing wrong.

My client, a large toy company, had a brand that had been selling quite well for two years, but was beginning to fade. Something had to be done. They devised a promotion to give a kick to sales early in the summer. It was a banded pack so that kids could get two of this collectible item for the price of one. The timing was crucial, so that the trade would see sales movement before the next year's selling season began in August.

We advertised the promotion on TV, beginning six weeks after the promotional product was shipped from the client distribution centers. That was the normal time allowed for product to get into stores.

The advertising ran. Absolutely nothing happened. Not a blip on the sales chart, as the consumer sales figures continued their relentless downward trend. The clients roundly berated us for the miserable failure of our advertising and the brand itself was totally written off. That year was to be its last year of advertised sales.

Two months later, the usual bi-weekly report on consumer sales came out. It stated, "The special banded pack of Brand X is now beginning to appear on shelf." Our advertising had run when there was no promotional product on shelf, because no one had allowed time for existing (slow moving) product to clear, or arranged to replace it with the promotion. It's hard to persuade kids to buy something they can't actually get!

And another:

A Story from Sandy Wax

When I headed a market research group at Discovery Channel, we embarked on our first-ever international focus group project with both excitement and some trepidation. While this was the first time we would hear real viewers' reactions to our channel outside of the U.S., I had heard all the horror stories about local research firms who recruited family members as participants or maintained cramped focus group facilities with small boxes for observation rooms. We hired a research manager with experience in Latin America, and she contacted a research agency in Mexico City that she had used on a number of projects with her former employer. Using her perfect Spanish, my research manager communicated on a daily basis with the Mexican agency to make sure everything would run seamlessly.

When our entire senior management team got to the focus group facility in Mexico City, there was a party going on. While the agency had been doing business in Mexico for a number of years, they were excited to unveil their brand new state-of-the art focus group facility for us. Our team was impressed. In addition to having a ceremonial ribbon cutting complete with champagne, our hosts showed us a facility that was well designed and had all the newest technology. This was going to be great. We checked that the Spanish-English translators were there to interpret for the observers in the back room, and we were ready to go!

When the respondents entered the discussion room, we asked the facility to turn up the volume. Most of our cable execs did not speak Spanish, so we needed to get the sound turned on for the translators. A moment of panic ensued as technicians fiddled with knobs and adjusted microphones. The momentary panic switched to full-fledged dread when we realized there was no sound. Nothing. Our viewers were behind the mirror chatting animatedly about something, but we couldn't hear a word. Not in Spanish, nor English. Nothing. So our first international research project literally fell on deaf ears. The few Spanish speakers among us moved into the room with the participants (disguised as "note takers"). The rest of us rolled off to the hotel bar, where we interviewed the waiters and hotel guests about their experiences with Discovery Channel.

And another:

Anonymous Storyteller
How to kill a new product idea in research!
   No, this isn't a story about bad research. It's a misadventure that killed a raft of new ideas. Even now, I'm not sure how it could have been averted. Many years ago, a client in the confectionery business in the U.K. set out to evaluate a range of new product ideas. Some of them seemed to have very good potential. They took the ideas to focus groups across the country, and discovered that they had some possible hits. Hurray!
   About a week later, the marketing director received a phone call from his counterpart at one of the other huge confectionery companies (there are three which dominate the category in Britain). The caller described to him in detail what the concepts were that had been researched, and told him the results of the groups, killing any chance that these ideas could be developed further. The competitive edge was blown.
   What had gone wrong? Had someone in the research company or the advertising agency (or, worse still, the client) breached confidentiality?
   No. The answer was much simpler. When we screen for research, we always ask questions to ensure we don't get experts or competitors in the sample. "Do you, or any of your family work in advertising, marketing, the X business, public relations etc." (X being whatever category our client is in.) We don't ask, "Who is your next-door neighbor?"
   A lady in one of the groups was the next-door neighbor of the competitor's marketing director, and had simply told him in passing about the fun she had in our client's focus group, and the interesting ideas they were coming out with.
   Boom! End of the project.

   Lack of attention to important details can have consequences that are even more serious. The best selling book *The Darwin Awards* bestows dubious honors upon people who die while doing rather stupid things.

It recites one particular case where two construction workers were working aloft some one hundred feet above the ground. They cut a circular hole in a concrete slab, without realizing they were both standing in the center of the circle. They fell eight stories to their deaths.

THE PASSION TO OVERCOME OBSTACLES

History is filled with stories of great inventions and successes that were born of apparent serendipity—fortunate discoveries made accidentally. Columbus discovered a new continent while looking for an old one. Newton created his Law of Gravitation from the chance observation of an apple falling. Archimedes shouted "Eureka!" when he stepped into a tub of water and watched it overflow, thus helping him to solve a mathematical formula for estimating volume. Edward Jenner created the smallpox vaccine, having remembered that, as a boy of 19, a milkmaid told him that she could not get smallpox because she had already had cowpox. That led him to a grand idea years later—to inoculate people with cowpox so that they would be immune to smallpox.

The list is endless, with chance event after chance event seemingly contributing to accidental discoveries and the birth of entire industries.

Don't believe it. So-called "chance discoveries" hide a deeper truth. The people in these stories, and so many more, had something in common. Most were not novices in their fields. They were persistent. They gained valuable knowledge. They worked harder still, overcoming the odds until they found themselves in a position to take advantage of serendipity (yes, some of these people were undoubtedly workaholics).

They had passion, and that passion allowed them to competently succeed by overcoming even the greatest of hurdles.

The harder you work, the more persistent you are, the more luck you seem to have. It's an old adage. You will not work hard unless you are strongly, positively motivated. That will not happen unless you are first passionate about what you are doing.

There was a man who was a failure in business, so somewhere along the line he decided to run for a political office. He met with failure after failure in that endeavor, too. He was defeated for a seat in the State Legislature, defeated for a seat in the U.S. Congress several times, defeated for a seat in the U.S. Senate a couple of times, and was defeated for Vice President of the United States. Anyone else would have quit. In fact, I once attended a lecture by a noted psychology professor who talked about how to live a happier life, and his main thesis was that we should adjust our expectations to our abilities. I raised my hand and gave the example of the man I cite above. I asked the professor what advice he would give him. The professor said that the man simply was not cut out to be a politician, and that he should reevaluate what he is good at, where his abilities lay, and try something else. I had trapped the good professor (a nasty ploy) because the life story of the man above was that of Abraham Lincoln before he became President of the United States in 1860. Lincoln was one persistently Good Knight, who became an immortal Philosopher King.

Never discount passion and persistence. I believe in what I call the *Effort of 1000*. Simply put: billions of people in this world have benefited greatly due to the persistent passion, restless curiosity, attention to a task, and rare abilities of only 1,000 incredibly gifted people who have had an impact on medicine, politics, science, industry, and the arts. They overcame tremendous odds. Without them, the world would not be what it is today. If each of us could tap into a fragment of that same passion that is within all of us, what an even greater world we would have.

Yet there are more everyday stories to the contrary.

A Story by David Schneider

I moved from Detroit to Dallas to take a position as an engineer with a small military sub-contractor on a project that initially had a one-year timeline. By the time I came onto the project, a year had already passed and it was estimated that it would take another year to finish the job. So, after a year, they were a year behind! Because the military was concerned about the project's many delays, it alerted us that it would be sending a team of auditors to our facility to discuss the issues. The night before the audit team was to show up, Dallas had a small ice storm. Having just moved to Dallas from Detroit and being used to bad weather, I drove into work in the morning without thinking much about it. The auditors, having flown in the night before from

Washington D.C. (and with similar cold weather skills), showed up shortly after I did. What neither the auditors nor I realized was the extent to which the citizens of Dallas hate cold weather. Only 10 people at our company of 100 people came to work that day. The auditors realized that the project was far behind because of such little dedication.

PASSION TO CONFRONT KINGS

Just as some brave Knights find themselves in a position to guard kingdoms against unscrupulous Monarchs, it also happens that some brave Knights must guard kingdoms against incompetent Monarchs and their bureaucracies. This is not about illegality, but simple bad judgment on the part of the nobility. In most cases, this might entail a brief conversation with the nobility, perhaps a note outlining suggestions. At times, however, the risk to one's career can be grave, for pointing out incompetence and misjudgments can carry huge repercussions. Forget just bravery. This takes passion.

Yet that's precisely what Coleen Rowley did. As chief counsel in the Minneapolis field office of the FBI, Ms. Rowley blew the whistle on the organization she loves. She did so by writing a 13-page memo to FBI Director Robert Mueller outlining the ways in which the FBI might have helped disrupt the September 11th attack upon the World Trade Center, but did not. She also delivered the letter to the Senate Intelligence Committee, I imagine so that her concerns would not be buried. The letter detailed how, in advance of the tragedy, FBI headquarters dismissed the Minneapolis field office's observations and speculations regarding one of the alleged conspirators. Coleen Rowley told not only the King, but also the entire world, that the FBI did not handle the events with complete competence. That Knight has grit, born of endless passion. For an important, shining moment, she became the teacher, and her King the student.

A Knight's Code of Business

Passion: A Good Knight is passionate about the craft.

And Other Advice

Good Knights, hire people with a burning passion for their craft. Put them in the right jobs to take advantage of their skills and desires. Provide training opportunities to help them grow. If your Squires are not up to the task, you have yourself to blame, for you have either placed them in jobs not suited to their talents, or you have not given them suitable training. Ensure that you do not endorse the passion for riches instead of the passion for more noble pursuits. Some Evil Barons can be detected because they cannot hide their love of the former, as we have seen.

Good Squires-in-Training, be passionate about what you do, or at the very least, find something within what you do that you can be passionate about. If there is nothing there that excites you, find something else you can be passionate about, for you will never achieve competence in those endeavors in which you lack heart. Then never, ever stop learning. If your current Kingdom will not take the time to train you, find a Kingdom that will. It will make an immeasurable difference in your quest for knighthood. Be passionate about the details. If you are not, find someone who is. When screw-ups happen (they always happen), make amends, learn from it, and move on.

Good Monarchs, your kingdom depends upon passion. If you do not value it, recruit it, nurture it, and exhibit it yourself, your kingdom will not achieve its greatest.

Evil Barons, your passion for power and riches will likely be achieved in the short term, but will expose you in the long term, for the world is watching.

Chapter 10

Lack of a Visionary

"The future will tell, Sancho. Time, the discoverer of all things, leaves nothing that it does not drag into the light of the sun, even though it be buried in the bosom of the Earth."

—Don Quixote

Kingdoms are born, grow, and amass great wealth, and those within their realms prosper, when they embrace visionaries. Similarly, they shrink and become sickly, when those in power either have no vision themselves, or shun those that do.

INABILITY TO ACCEPT THE IMPOSSIBLE

Passion contributes mightily to competence. However, it is quite another thing to embrace the impossible. This is true of even great men and women who were in every other respect pillars of competence, expertise, and passion, but they lacked the vision to dream. Some examples:

"This 'telephone' has too many shortcomings to be seriously considered as a means of communication. The device is inherently of no value to us."
—Western Union internal memo, 1876

"I have traveled the length and breadth of this country and talked with the best people, and I can assure you that data processing is a fad that won't last out the year."
—The editor in charge of business books for Prentice Hall, 1957

"While theoretically and technically television may be feasible, commercially and financially it is an impossibility."
—Lee DeForest, inventor

"This concept is interesting and well-formed, but in order to earn better than a 'C', the idea must be feasible."
—A Yale University management professor's comments on Fred Smith's new business idea (Smith founded Federal Express)

"Radio has no future. Heavier-than-air flying machines are impossible. X-rays will prove to be a hoax."
—William Thomson (Lord Kelvin), English scientist, 1899

Here are my two favorites:
"It will be years—not in my time—before a woman will become Prime Minister."
—Margaret Thatcher, 1974 (later to become Prime Minister)

"There is not the slightest indication that nuclear energy will ever be obtainable. It would mean that the atom would have to be shattered at will."
—Albert Einstein, 1932

Thank goodness, someone is keeping track.

These brilliant people could not, for the moment, accept the impossible. If *they* could not see it, what hope is there for the rest of us? Quotes such as those from Margaret Thatcher are particularly inspiring, however, and offer hope, because they demonstrate that one's beliefs can change, and in so doing, we can transform the world and ourselves.

A LACK OF VISIONARIES

Some business books talk about "visionary companies" and pay only lip service to the flesh and blood visionary. That is unfortunate. For there can be no visionary company without the visionary person.

Unfortunately, some corporations have no flesh and blood visionaries.

◥ SURVEY OF 100

Forty-two percent of our survey completely agreed that their company has a true visionary, someone who can take their organization to the next level; 41 percent agreed only somewhat, suggesting they are not all that convinced; 14 percent disagreed; 3 percent did not know or refused to answer.

Fifty-four percent agreed completely that their company has a clear vision or mission as to where it is headed; 32 percent agreed only somewhat; 14 percent disagreed.

Those in charge of companies without visionaries or visions are more often caretakers, having inherited the company from other caretakers, and so on. They may be quite good at it, and turn a handsome profit, but they are not apt to break truly new ground.

Upward competence is about vision, and visionaries.

VISIONARIES IN ACTION

While on the advertising agency side, I worked with a few clients who had truly an inspiring visionary and vision. The one I recall most was that of Microsoft. Bill Gates's vision was simple and bold: *a computer on every desk and in every home.* To those working on the business, those few words were immensely motivating. Contrast the Gates's vision with another sage of the same era:

> *"There is no reason anyone would want a computer in their home.*
> —Ken Olsen, president, chairman and founder of
> Digital Equipment Corp., 1977

These are two men of important stature and intelligence and passion and apparent competence. However, one dreamed the impossible.

That's what a visionary does. That's what a vision is. It scares the heck out of 99 percent of the rest of us who will never have a vision of our own, or if we do, will not have the wherewithal to know what to do about it. Visionaries kick us in the backside until we believe. As part of Microsoft's advertising agency team, we had to ponder . . . *just what in the heck must we all do to achieve a computer on every desk and in every home?* How could our small advertising contributions, even combined with the might of Microsoft product development, make that possible? The answer was obvious. Only by making products that deliver real benefits in people's everyday lives, and by communicating these benefits in such a way that consumers will understand Microsoft's immense, positive role in their lives, would this be possible. The vision was tangible enough for those of us without vision to understand. We knew where to march, even though we could not be sure we would ever reach the vision. How many homes have computers? How many desks? What can we do this year to up that by 10 percent, and the next year, and the next? *Advertising Age* recently noted that Microsoft is about to embark on an endeavor by "positioning the software giant as an enabler of personal and professional creative potential." It sounds like the march to put a computer on every desk and in every home continues.

A computer on every desk and in every home was not some lofty goal. It had teeth. A lofty goal would have been a proclamation that Microsoft aims to be the *best* software developer. I have seen those mission statements a thousand times, and every time they prove too vague.

I suppose that John F. Kennedy could have said that the United States was going to have the *best* space program, and left it at that. That would have made us all feel good, and our country would have defined *best* in any way we wanted to suit the times and our meager capabilities. It would have left a lot of wiggle room, but Kennedy did not. Instead, he said: "This nation should commit itself to achieving the goal, before this decade is out, of landing a man on the Moon and returning him safely to the Earth." He wanted a vision that scared us, one that would make those in the space program work their tails off to achieve. Had Kennedy done otherwise, is there any doubt that the Russians would have gotten to the moon first? When Kennedy made his proclamation, the USSR was far ahead.

INVISIBLE DOORS

Visionaries take you places that did not exist before they arrived—no doors proclaimed "This way!"

Her name was Ruth Mosko, the daughter of Polish immigrants who came to the United States aboard a steamship many years ago. This was a very humble beginning for a woman who would become one of the most famous toy inventors of all time. Ruth Mosko created a brand that many generations of girls would call their own. Ruth Mosko, later known as Ruth Handler, invented Barbie.

At a time when baby dolls ruled and playing *mother* was what girls were expected to do, Ruth had a vision. She reached beyond society's customs of that day and into the future when girls could aspire to be anything they wanted to be. Barbie became a conduit to a vast assortment of dreams. While Barbie began life as a teenage fashion model of sorts, she soon became a nurse, a doctor, a business executive, an astronaut, and even President of the United States. Ruth Handler saw something others did not. She saw where girls were, and wondered aloud where their limitless dreams might take them. Some critics of Barbie think she represents unobtainable expectations, and they focus upon her beauty, her shapely figure, and her blonde hair. The critics judge Barbie by her looks (shouldn't do that in this day and age!), and in so doing, they ignore her Olympic achievements and college degrees. Girls don't.

The "vision" of Barbie was immense because it fueled young girls' power to dream, to touch their futures in ways that were not possible before Barbie arrived. Today there are women doctors, astronauts, and CEO's. I'm willing to bet that many of them played with Barbie at a time when little girls were not expected to enter these professions. Barbie was there first, leading the way. Have your business and your visionaries had that profound affect on society? Few have.

Mattel is the company Barbie built, and it remains so today despite more ups and downs than a jester's dunking stool.

I worked on the Barbie brand for 17 years and while I never had the pleasure of meeting Ruth Handler, I did come to know another of Mattel's visionaries, despite a fiasco that wounded her later. Her name is Jill Barad.

When I started working at Ogilvy & Mather in 1981, one of my first presentations was to our Mattel client, Jill Barad, who was a lowly product manager at the time. My last presentation before leaving Ogilvy & Mather in 1998 was also to Jill. During the time in between, Jill rose from the ranks of junior marketing executive to CEO. The brand that she affected most was Barbie. During Jill's reign Barbie grew from about

$200 million dollars in sales to a nearly $2 billion dollar brand, making it one of the most successful toys of all time. While many people can share credit for that accomplishment, Jill was the brand steward who often mattered most. Jill had a powerful combination of refined intelligence and creative intuition. Many people never, ever achieve that, because these are innate gifts. Jill can see things no one else can see, especially in product and in advertising. In meeting after meeting, we could see her mind bubble with marketing ideas that would take products and advertising to the next level.

Many of those contributions are overlooked these days because during Jill's reign, Mattel paid literally billions of dollars for a children's software publisher called The Learning Company that in time was without value. That was a woeful misadventure. Jill lost her job soon thereafter. I don't know if Jill's passion ran beyond good sense, or if others swayed her to do things beyond her judgment, or if she didn't have the benefit of a strong financial partner with the authority to tell her "Stop!" My hunch it was the latter. However, I do know that visionaries have their strengths and weaknesses, glories and disasters. Jill had all of these.

VISIONARIES WITHOUT PARTNERS INVITE MISADVENTURES

Which brings up an important point: Powerful visionaries must be balanced with an equally powerful company manager (a visionary manager), someone who knows the mechanics of business, who can build an effective organization around the vision, and who has the power to confront the visionary himself, to keep the company from being inadvertently steered into rough misadventures. It's a delicate balance to strike. If the visionary has too much power, the company may take risks that are too big. If the manager has too much power, the company will stagnate and the visionary will leave. While visionaries are often credited with the spark that created companies and industries, it has been documented repeatedly that they are not necessarily the right people to manage companies. That's a different kind of visionary, one who knows how to manage the vision.

The best balance often exists when both the visionary and the manager share power, and each recognizes and appreciates the contributions of the other. The most striking combinations in the past several decades include Disney's Michael Eisner and Frank Wells (not forgetting Walt and Roy), and Hewlett and Packard. These combinations are extremely rare, yet oh so valuable.

My wife and I dabble in the stock market (not something many us care to admit anymore). We found a medium-sized company that seemed to have greater potential. Its stock price had recently crashed even more than the market averages, and it tossed its CEO. It looked like a good time to buy. I had hopes the company would hire a visionary, so we bought a little stock. The new CEO showed up. My wife and I went to the first shareholder's meeting to see if he was a visionary. He seemed to be a very competent manager, but I kept looking for the visionary type who would take the business to a new level. The new guy did not have it, nor did the people around him. They were all caretakers, and probably good ones, but no one scared us just enough to believe in the impossible. My wife and I sold our stock. To this day, the share price remains lethargic.

THE VISIONARY INSIDE

Visionaries are not just people we read about in the headlines. They are among us, everyday, if only we recognize them.

I know a man named Larry. He is a visionary of sorts. Some know it. Some might disagree with this assessment. He ran the direct marketing division for an agency in Los Angeles many years ago and built it from nothing to a large concern. He went on to be co-chairman of an agency office in China, and is now a president with another agency there. Like Jill Barad, Larry is smart, with both a keen intellect and a strong creative bent. During a pitch for a new business in Los Angeles years ago, Larry decided that the question the client was asking us to address was not the real issue the company should be worried about. I will put aside all the details for the sake of brevity. Larry decided to address the assignment the client had given us, but to go one step further and present a far grander vision of what the company could be.

We pitched the business. The client was a bit nervous about the vision, but we won, and did great work for them.

Larry has a knack for seeing the future (and sometimes getting it right, which is more than the rest of us can say). He also has a habit of making people angry, which is why I think he's worth pointing out. Larry sometimes pushed and pushed until people did not want to be pushed any more. He hates bureaucracies. Wherever Larry went in the early days, he seemed to bring controversy. Some might even have said that he was an Evil Baron, particularly in his youth, though I think otherwise. He's smart, his mind is always bubbling with ideas, and yes, he can be confrontational at times. He has all the hallmarks of other everyday visionaries I have known, like Gary, Brad, Jerry, Bill and a host of others (you know who you are). While they don't always make the headlines, they do see things that others do not. Their minds are always restless. They see opportunity everywhere. Constantly. They want to transform companies and industries to help them reach new levels.

Unfortunately, sometimes the opportunities that everyday visionaries see require bureaucracies to change their ways and adapt to new environments and conditions, often by changing the very way the bureaucracy is structured. That can make for a bumpy road.

All of our companies have everyday visionaries. The trick is to recognize them, tolerate them, and believe, just for a moment, that they might be on to something. Unfortunately, some companies believe they have to hire visionaries from the outside, because they don't believe they have them inside the company. Most of the time that is a waste, because they have visionaries right under their noses but do not recognize them as such. Yet, the visionaries they hire from the outside are no better than those within, and in many cases, are worse because they do not understand the corporate culture of the company they are joining. The board of directors simply thinks they are better, and then pays an enormous sum to entice them. In the book *Good to Great* by Jim Collins, the author discovered that *"larger-than-life, celebrity leaders who ride in from the outside are negatively correlated with taking a company from good to great."* Then how are these "celebrity leaders" hired? Good PR people, an aristocracy that believes PR, and an innate unwillingness to believe in your own visionaries.

THE GRAND VISIONARY DILEMMA

You don't have to be a rocket scientist to be a visionary. The quotes in the beginning of the chapter attest that even rocket scientists are not necessarily visionaries. You simply have to dream "what if." Moreover, if you can't dream "what if," you have to be willing to open yourself up to those who can. This is a grand dilemma. All of our training tells us not to believe in the crackpot visionary, and yet we have to muster the faith to believe that maybe, just maybe, the visionary is right. This is not easy, and it is made more complicated by the fact that there are plenty of so-called visionaries who have been wrong.

Visionaries make us nervous, because following a vision carries risks to our jobs, careers, institutions, and to our sanity. There is no easy solution. However, if you don't embrace *any* visionary, while you may still prosper, you will never reach the moon, or inspire little girls to dream, or put a computer on every desk and in every home. Never.

A Knight's Code of Business

Vision: A Good Knight protects and cultivates the visionaries, for they are the future of the realm.

And Other Advice

Good Knights, strive to believe in things you cannot see, but use open debate to identify the potential glories and disasters that may accrue if you adopt particular visions. Only experience can help you here.

Good Squires-in-Training, keep an open mind. "Training" can sometimes inadvertently condition us to accept only what seems possible based upon historical observations, while preventing us from seeing the impossible. There are no impossibilities.

Good Monarchs, learn to identify visionaries. They do not take small steps as most of us do, but big leaps that frighten us all. Marry the visionary to a good business manager who appreciates visions, and watch as the two bring riches to the kingdom.

Visionaries, if you are a visionary, live only within the kingdom that appreciates your value, for any other kingdom will bring death to your spirit.

Chapter 11

Communication Scarcity

"There, there you are, Sancho! On you go, threading, tacking, and stitching together proverb after proverb till nobody can make head or tail of you."
—Don Quixote

~

If yours is a lucky kingdom, you have an abundance of people with high moral character. You have people who are passionate about their craft. You have put them in the right roles to take advantage of their talents. In addition, you have a visionary who can take your kingdom to great heights, never before imagined.

However, if you cannot communicate well with those inside and outside your company, you are lost and incompetent, for the kingdom depends upon ample, articulate communications. Charles E. Young, former Chancellor of UCLA, told the author of the book *If I Knew Then What I Know Now*, "Vision, determination, and hard work are not always enough. Failure sometimes means simply that others do not share your dreams."

It all begins with communicating those dreams. Unfortunately, many companies either do not employ a town crier, or they inadvertently shoot the one they do employ.

NON-PROCLAIMED PROCLAMATIONS

Visions are to be proclaimed. Proclamations set the tone and provide a common set of objectives by which the empire will grow and flourish.

Unfortunately, in today's business realms, too few corporate proclamations are designed and fewer still are communicated to the kingdom.
Therefore, the subjects, in turn, know too little about the overall corporate mission or vision, and hence, how their contributions can help
achieve corporate ends.

 SURVEY OF 100

Only 26 percent completely agreed that most employees in their
company are fully aware of the company's vision or mission; 44
percent agreed only somewhat that their employees were aware;
30 percent disagreed that most people in their companies are
fully aware of the company's vision or mission.

These are misadventures in progress. Here is a story about a division that either had no vision, or if it did, those in charge could not
communicate what it was.

A Story by Gary Elliott

*A team of consultants had the task of uncovering the strategic
direction and competency of a multi-billion dollar division so that
they could prepare a marketing recommendation. Many interviews
with senior people from all over the world produced little understanding of how this division was organized or the vision behind it. It
seemed as if there was no connection to any of the pieces. After months,
they finally got an hour with the president of this division—the guy
with the answers. He had been there for years; knew the formula for
success and why it all made sense. After appropriate warm-up, he was
asked for his perspective on what made this division tick and what
opportunities and pitfalls lay before it. He spent the next 50 minutes
describing the origins of the universe—atoms colliding, the development of sea and land animals, human life, etc. As time was running
short, he was again pressed for his views on a vision and essence.
"Look," he said, "it all comes down to $100 a share; you guys go fig-
ure out how to get there."*

These are not small matters, for as this story demonstrates, it can happen at the top of mammoth organizations where billions of dollars, and potentially thousands of jobs, are at stake. How is any Knight supposed to lead troops into battle when the Monarch cannot articulate a vision, supported by a clear roadmap on how to achieve it?

You cannot. Hence, the kingdom does not reach its full potential. Many kingdoms are successful in spite of themselves, not because of themselves.

Proclaimed Proclamations

John F. Kennedy communicated his vision of landing a man on the moon to the world. The proclamation was critical *because it obligated those in the space program and the government to achieve those ends,* while at the same time soliciting support from the entire nation. "Let it be clear," he said, "that I am asking the Congress and the country to accept a firm commitment to a new course of action—a course which will last for many years and carry heavy costs.... If we are to go only half way, or reduce our sights in the face of difficulty, in my judgment, it would be better not to go at all." Kennedy told us what was needed. He outlined the costs. He urged the nation to get on board, and to stay there until the task was done. It would have been too embarrassing, and politically disastrous, to do otherwise.

Similarly, Microsoft communicated its proclamation—*a computer on every desk and in every home*—to everybody. You would have had to be sealed in a chamber during the last two decades to have not come across that statement. When our advertising agency crafted an overall positioning for Microsoft in the 1980s in support of that grand vision, we put the positioning statement on each and every advertising strategy. No matter how minute the program or product was, we left a space for the account executive to explain how his or her small effort contributed to the overall brand positioning and vision. It made us think, and more than one advertising strategy was sent back for retooling. It ensured that every piece of communication fed into the larger communication, so that there would be no misunderstanding. It was clear and focused.

Every soul that works for Disney knows that a core objective is to make people happy. Disney is relentless in its desire that every Guest (what other companies call customers) leaves with a smile. They communicate this idea to their Cast Members (i.e. employees) through training seminars, in newsletters, and so on. It's simple. It's exacting. It's powerful. Because Disney creates well-articulated, simple objectives, it makes it easier to orchestrate the entire organization behind the same goal. It can even have an impact on hiring practices, to ensure that the Cast Members have the right kind of passion, one that supports the brand objective of making guests happy.

Alternatively, some companies guard their visions, missions, and objectives as they guard their patented formulas. They are too afraid to let even their employees see them. Rubbish. A good vision statement not only inspires employees, it throws fear into the hearts of competitors. Some companies' vision statements never make it past the pages of the annual report. They are more for show, to make investors believe that there is a mission when in truth it is simply wallpaper to impress the visitors.

Shared Visions

The strength of the kingdom is not solely in the Monarch's ability to communicate a vision, but also in the Monarch's ability to listen to the royal subjects to gain their insights for the vision. For wise Monarchs know that they can learn much from those within their realms, and that upward communication is the way to achieve that learning. There is more. Insights gained from those across the realm can help create a powerful *shared* vision for the organization as a whole and kingdoms can prosper as a result.

Anne Sweeney is president of ABC Cable Networks Group, which includes responsibility for Disney Channel, Toon Disney, SoapNet, and ABC's interests in Lifetime, A&E, the History Channel, and E! Entertainment Television. In order to set worldwide direction for several of the Disney branded networks, Ms. Sweeney beckoned some 50 knights from distant corners of the kingdom to meet face to face. The sole purpose was to hear each other's words and discover each other's insights, in order to craft grand brand visions. It was a Knight's Roundtable, and a visionary one at that.

I had the good fortune of moderating a couple of these round-tables, in the role of independent court arbiter. My job was simply to ensure that all voices and insights were heard. They were, and the knowl-edge proved invaluable. It was used to craft worldwide visions. Those who helped create the visions then implemented them around the world. Hence, the visions were not dictated from above, but created by valuable insights from those below. That fostered "ownership" among those who had to implement the visions and the kingdom greatly bene-fitted as a result.

In the book *Good to Great,* author Jim Collins discovered that great leaders "first got the right people on the bus," and then "figured out where to drive it." The process is simple: Get good people, bring them together, learn from them, let them help craft a vision, and then make it happen. Teamwork at its best.

It's all about communication. It works.

BREAKING DOWN WALLS

A couple years before I left Ogilvy & Mather to start my own consul-tancy, CEO Shelly Lazarus instituted a routine procedure she called "long hallways." It was a process whereby she would take human resources and expertise from one office and send them to benefit a client in another office. Hence, no matter where the client was located, it could tap into strengths of Ogilvy around the world. I was one of the people launched into Shelly's long hallways. I saw it work for clients as agency teams from around the globe descended upon a client's busi-ness to help craft brand strategies and communications. It broke down the geography that can inadvertently separate a kingdom into a feudal system, and allowed clients to get the resources they needed, wherever those resources might be. As a company, I saw Ogilvy become closer, tighter, and more connected. Shelly continues to expand upon the idea even today to meet challenges of global brands in global markets. "We continue to take away geography," Shelly told me. "That's because geography is irrelevant. Where people live is irrelevant. Our objective is to provide the best brains in the world no matter where they are." Some agencies might give this lip service, but they don't routinely institute it. Ogilvy has used this process to help immense clients like IBM gain the resources they needed to craft and communicate brand visions to the world.

Breaking down walls is really about opening communications among offices and getting office heads to share knowledge and goals. Only then can resources be shared and allocated accordingly.

ALL COMMUNICATIONS, LARGE AND SMALL

Beyond the big misadventures that might ensue due to an inability to communicate, companies and individuals face many lesser, routine misadventures.

 SURVEY OF 100

Only 18 percent completely agreed that the level of day-to-day internal communications in their company is excellent; 43 percent agreed somewhat, suggesting it is not what it should be; 38 percent disagreed; 1 percent refused or did not know.

A misadventure in hiring A huge division within a Fortune 500 company was growing rapidly. The human resources department was hiring madly for months to fill many spots. They needed shiny new Knights and Squires-in-Training, and Serfs, and Princesses. Once hired, they were given offices and manuals and training began. It was glorious. Unfortunately, the accountants in this great realm never told human resources that the company was about to announce a record loss, and that the company was about to downsize significantly. In one month's time, the hundreds that had been hired were suddenly fired, at great expense to all. The division was out of business soon thereafter.

A misadventure in optimism Many years ago, a large office in a worldwide company was cutting staff. It had to. It had lost business, profits were down, and workload was down. They let a couple dozen people go, and then proclaimed to those lucky enough to remain, "This was the end of it. We can get back to work and not have to worry about more cuts!"

It was an inspiring speech. However, within 6 months another layoff ensued, and management gave the same speech. "Really," they said. "This is the end of it this time. No more cuts after this. We are not kidding this time. Really. We mean it. Really we do."

Few believed management the second time. Some thought they had actually lied when, after the first cut, they said it was the end of the layoffs. In point of fact, they had not lied. However, they were guilty of unjustified optimism, which they communicated to the staff in abundance. They tried so hard to bolster confidence and morale after the first cut that trust was inadvertently broken when more layoffs were needed. It took time before people would trust management proclamations again. I know, as I was part of that management, part of the morale boosters, part of the cheerleading squad, and hence, part of the problem. After that, I took more care in what I said, and what I promised. I learned the hard way.

A misadventure one-to-one Once upon a time there were two Good Knights. Both were quite skilled in their respective disciplines, both were respected by their King and their Squires, and both were even respected by other Kings who knew of their skills. Unfortunately, each of these Good Knights, working in the same kingdom, believed that the other was an Evil Baron. Why? Because each Good Knight had different department objectives, which were sometimes in conflict. It was not good for the kingdom.

They did not see themselves as competitors, for that would have been even worse. Neither Knight had taken the time to understand the issues and the problems that the other faced. Neither had taken the time to open the barriers that stood between them. This turned out to be a communications issue. Then one day, an Arbiter Knight who knew both Good Knights took it upon himself to talk to each, and to explain that each was, in fact, another Good Knight. The Good Knights were skeptical.

"Can't be!" they shouted.

"Yet it is!" explained the Arbiter Knight.

Both Knights agreed to communicate, to share objectives, and to try to understand each other's issues and needs. And so it came to pass. Then some months later, the Good Knights came to the Arbiter Knight, and thanked him for his intervention, and all in the kingdom rejoiced.

It is all about communication. The more you take the time to understand the motives and needs of others, the more you will be able to find common ground.

TO LISTEN, YOU GOTTA HEAR

Some misadventures occur because while some executives appear to *listen*, they do not really *hear*. Or if they hear, they eventually *ignore*.

Anonymous Storyteller

We're invited to the pitch based on our reputation. The potential client is most interested in creative solutions. "Show us some great creative. Can't wait! See you."

The pitch is assembled, the creative is great, we are ready to wow them. I'm a confident Creative Director.

Pitch day. We've got two hours.

The management and account people show them who we are, where we are, what we do, what we think. But enough about us. Let's talk about our clients! List our clients, what have we done for them, creative that has solved their problems, creative that has won awards, ideas that were terrific. Discussion, discussion. And now for the creative solutions to your *problems.*

Them: But we have to go.

Us: OK, fine, take this booklet. You'll love the stuff.

We never saw them again.

You have to give your clients, customers, and consumers what they ask for. It is a very simple principle. Yet many suppliers give customers what *they* want to deliver, regardless of what is desired.

FOCUS, FOCUS, FOCUS

Focused messages are best. It doesn't matter if you are giving a speech to the World Trade Organization or to your local PTA. Yet too often we try too hard to communicate too much, and consequently, we communicate nothing. As compared with this:

Veni, vidi, vici — I came, I saw, I conquered

I once worked with a company that launched several new products each year. They fell in love with the naming process. The names for many of these new products were colorful, inspiring, fun, and *five words long!* We conducted a study to see if anyone could recall the names when exposed to the various brands' television commercials. Sure enough, the longer the name was the smaller the percentage of people that could remember it. No one recalled the longest names. In fact, even the people who showed interest in the brands did not know what to ask for when they went to the store! That was unfortunate, since all of the names were fixed at that point, and nothing could be done about it.

To see how focused a company's internal communications are, just look at the advertising they implement for the rest of us. Is their advertising clear? Does it tell you the benefits of the brand or company? Does it tell you why it can deliver those benefits better than others can? Advertising, at its best, is that simple. But like all other things discussed in this book, companies make it harder than it needs to be.

"The best approach to take in our over-communicated society is the oversimplified message," so cautions Ries and Trout in their book *Positioning, The Battle for Your Mind.* Few listen. Those that do achieve much. I have had the great fortune to know many of them as well.

A Knight's Code of Business

Communication: A Good Knight listens carefully and communicates carefully to all those within the realm and beyond, in an honest and concise way.

And Other Advice

Good Knights, you must break down walls—among departments, across geography, across titles, across rank—so that communications flow in all directions.

Good Squires-In-Training, first and foremost, learn to listen. Understand issues before you speak. That's the only way you can render the appropriate aid to those who need it. You must also learn to think and communicate clearly. Thinking and communicating are linked, for confused communications are an indicator of confused thinking. If these are not remedied early in a career, a Squire's chance of becoming a Knight is severely diminished.

Good Monarchs, communicate bold visions to the world. Internally, designate an Arbiter Knight and make it his or her job to inspire communications, to settle disputes, to bring Good Knights together. A little process can be important here. Beware of those who are unwilling to share information or lend aid to others in the kingdom, for Evil Barons tend to horde their knowledge and resources even when others in your kingdom are in dire need. Get rid of them, or your kingdom will never achieve its best.

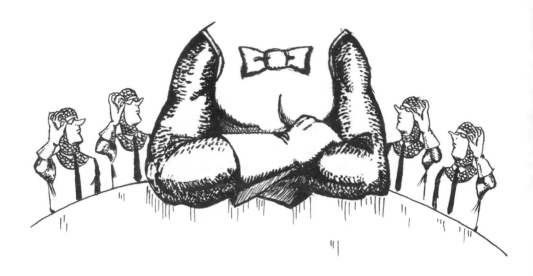

Chapter 12

Mediocrity

"Today sloth triumphs over industry, idleness over labor, vice over virtue, arrogance over bravery, and theory over the practice of arms, which only lived and flourished in the Golden Age and among knights-errant."

—DON QUIXOTE

~

To avoid misadventures and best another kingdom in the game of commerce, Knights need passion, vision, and communication. Moreover, while these are necessary to achieve competence, they are insufficient, for there is another demon that conspires against us. That demon is within us. We settle too early, too often, for less than we can be. We might have a clear vision, but do we have the will to make it come true? We push far, but not far enough. We come within striking distance of success, but fail to capture it. When we can't, mediocrity is the result. Those who have the ability to execute great plans tower over the rest of us.

Jack Welch, former CEO of GE had a vision for his company to "search out and participate in real growth industries and insist upon being number one or number two in every business they are in—the number one or number two leanest, lowest-cost, worldwide producers of quality goods and services." That would have been merely some lofty goal, except that he meant it. He instituted a strategy of "fix, sell, or close" to ensure that his vision was achieved. Without the force to implement visions, and to keep them on track, they dissipate and create mediocrity.

This chapter is about mediocrity and inferiority that can arise due to deficits in any of the aforementioned qualities of character or competence. It results in "me too" brands and "me too" companies and "me too" levels of competence and "me too" kingdoms. This is not to say that companies and executives do not know how to create superior brands. Most do. As always, things and people sometimes get in the way of greatness.

We often deceive ourselves into believing that our products are superior. Look at the following data. It says that marketers all across the United States believe that their company makes objectively better products than their competitors. Though you have to admire marketers' spin, they are wrong. They cannot *all* be better. If you ask consumers (which I often do), they tell us that many products are, in fact, alike, and to prove it, they trade off quite a bit between brands when a new coupon arrives in the mail.

 SURVEY OF 100

Sixty-four percent completely agreed that their company, objectively, makes better products or provides better services than competitive companies; 31 percent agreed somewhat; and only 3 percent disagreed; 2 percent did not know or refused to answer.

The generally accepted "hit" rate for new products is about 10 percent, meaning that 90 percent of new products fail in the marketplace. How objectively superior is that? My take: we want to believe we make superior products when in fact we really don't as viewed by those who must buy them. In this matter, we are delusional, much like Don Quixote himself.

Let us now look at some of the common elements that make our companies mediocre.

NOT DELIVERING ON GREAT VISIONS MAKES US MEDIOCRE

Long ago and far away, a novice Squire (me) worked on a packaged goods account at a time when new products were king, when shelf space was still growing, and dynasties were carved. One of my first assignments was to track a glorious new brand introduced by the kingdom. It was one of the firsts of its kind, an instant meal. Just add water and poof . . . mealtime. The product was marvelous, stupendous, visionary, and a new jewel of the kingdom. It was introduced to consumers with the fanfare given to all births of noble blood. Sales were way up after the launch. People were promoted and careers were secured.

My task was to review tracking results to help us dissect the *nature* of the sales. One tool was a diary panel, comprised of regular consumers who were recruited to record their grocery purchases. It would help the kingdom ascertain the types of people who purchased our new brand, their family composition, whether this was the first time they had purchased the brand (known as *Triers*), or a second time (known as *Repeaters*), and onward.

It turned out that the bulk of sales were from first time *Triers*. Few households, having tasted the product, were brave enough to try it again. Hence, there were few *Repeaters*. As soon the available pool of *Triers* was exhausted in the United States, sales began to fall. Great vision. Bad follow through. The product tasted lousy. I announced the news to the kingdom. It was like telling the king that not only was he naked, he smelled bad, too. I survived, but the brand did not.

During the brand's death throes, people who were involved in earlier product development told me that they knew the product formulation was not ready, but that it was rushed to market because the concept was so strong. Soon after the failure, an abundance of other companies entered the fray with better products, and gained a foothold that remains to this very day. Haste makes our businesses incompetently inferior. So does not fulfilling expectations. The vision was there. Success was within reach. However, the execution was poor. Mediocrity would have been a blessing, I suppose. Instead, we achieved inferiority (relative to expectations) and failure.

New story. Same kingdom. One year later. I was still a junior Squire. I was asked to present the results of a new product test designed to ascertain if the product showed sufficient volume potential to warrant introduction into a full test market that cost millions of dollars. I gave my presentation regarding the brand's potential—it had some—and then faded into the back of the room to watch and learn. There were all the department heads, Good Knights all, representing product development, marketing, research, finance, promotions, advertising, and so on. They debated every aspect of the brand's potential strengths and weaknesses. Did it really have a strong point of difference or not? Was it truly better than competitive products? Could it be mass-produced at the desired costs?

After the merits of the brand were examined, the head of the division, our Monarch, then addressed each department head directly, one at a time, and asked if his or her individual decision was a "go" or "no go." His eyes swept around the roundtable, falling hard on each person. In effect, he was giving each Good Knight the opportunity to raise a red flag in an open and non-judgmental forum. He was also marking the moment, so that all would remember that he was giving each a chance to stop the test market launch. To a person, all said, "Go!"

I smiled as I walked away from that meeting so many years ago, thinking to myself, "Yes, that's how it should be done!" Develop great visions. Follow through with great executions. Do not settle for mediocrity. Test them. Debate them. Then decide.

I worked in the toy industry for many years, and saw consumer return rates as high as 20 percent and more for products that simply did not work or were disappointing, lending a crushing blow to the brand and the companies that made them. Mediocrity and inferiority do not pay the highest dividend, at least in the long run. Superiority does. It can be tricky, though, for superiority is not just about some objective measure, but about subjective measures as well. When The Coca-Cola Company introduced New Coke, they had thousands of taste tests behind them that said New Coke tasted better. However, loyal Coke consumers do not just taste ingredients. They taste heritage and loyalty. Therefore, they rebelled, and refused to accept New Coke as a substitute for the brand they loved. It appears that the original formula's most valuable ingredient is its emotional connection to loyal users.

Dove Beauty Bars contain one-quarter moisturizing lotion. Mercedes has excellent engineering. Rice Krispies makes a fun sound. MTV rocks. These "features" lead to emotional connections, e.g. I feel beautiful. I feel accomplished. I feel happy. I feel cool. Is it any wonder these brands survive? They created not small, but big points of difference that mattered to their consumers on both a rational and emotional level. *Then they delivered.* Some companies do not have the vision, or the passion, or the persistence to do this so they stay stuck in the middle. They are good enough to stay afloat, but not good enough to rise to the top.

MEDIOCRE PRICING AND QUALITY MAKES US MEDIOCRE

I am forever in awe of how business folks underestimate the willingness of consumers to pay extra cash for better products. In meeting after meeting, I have heard this, "We can't add that feature to the brand because it will raise the cost by 10 cents. If we raise the price to cover it, our brand will be the most expensive. Then our sales will fall and we won't make our profit goal!"

I always reply, "That assumes your consumers will not be willing to pay more for a better product. Shouldn't we test it to ascertain if consumers will be willing to pay more?" In 99 percent of the cases, the debate stops there. The price is never tested, or not adequately. The new feature is never added. The brand stays forever mediocre with the same kinds of products as the competitor's, with the same kinds of features, and the same price. Sameness.

Yet brave companies have proven that consumers are willing to pay more for new features with benefits (rational or emotional) they desire. I often buy a nearly $4 cup of coffee at Starbucks. I love the taste, and I like the coffee house environment. Just imagine for a moment, if ten years ago a man walked into a major food company with a proposition to start a company that sells a $4 cup of high-quality coffee in a European-style coffee bar, even though the consumer can make an inferior one for pennies a cup at home. He would have been laughed out of the meeting (maybe this did happen). "No one will pay nearly $4 for a cup for coffee, you moron!"

Wrong.

Here's a story that is all too tragic. It relates how the incompetence of an anointed Prince can bring doom for all, particularly when that inept Prince mistakenly brings inadequate business models from one kingdom to another, thus spreading mediocrity everywhere he goes.

Anonymous Storyteller
High-Tech Hubris

For a very long time I believed that no one person in a sizeable corporation (other than the CEO) could make or break the enterprise. Whenever employees complained about how much damage an incompetent executive was doing, my approach would simply be to let the clock run out on that person, believing that no truly unfixable damage could be done by any one person. I believed in checks and balances, and I believed the system was designed to spread authority beyond any individual's ability to put a company's core competency at risk.

Was I ever proven wrong! Under significant market pressure from competitive entries in our categories, the high-tech company where I was a product development executive hired a senior vice president of sales and marketing from the packaged goods industry. After just a few months on the job, he inarguably concluded that our problems were entirely an issue of pricing. He looked at our primary competitor driving a strategy of high-volume, low-price and concluded that we were in a war for market share. We at that time were in a lower-volume, high-price market positioning, selling premium products at a premium-price point. The equity markets had tremendously rewarded our high gross margins and lauded our seemingly unending string of industry awards for creativity, quality, and innovation.

Well, the new SVP managed to convince our board that we were doing it all wrong, that software was no different from laundry detergent, that market share meant everything and high volume at lower margin would drive future earnings. His first winter holiday at the helm, he positioned our wholesale pricing such that retail prices could be reduced by 50 percent, all in one move. We doubled volume that quarter, and due to our historically high cost of R&D, improved earnings by less than 1 percent. With that earnings release, our market cap was cut in half. Ninety days later, volume was stable and so were earnings; no improvement, we had found our new scale. Our stock price *was halved again, forcing us to cut product development costs and lay off talent. Our next crop of lower-investment products failed creatively and commercially. No incremental sales, no awards.*

A year later, we were bought by the same competitor who had baited us to adopt their strategy. Not coincidentally, another year later the consolidated company was sold to an even larger company, which soon discovered that the entity was not producing any profits of any kind. The larger company subsequently wrote down almost the entire investment.

Can one person make a difference for the better or worse? Not any person, but the right person sure can be wrong. The perfect formula of a little arrogance matched with just enough ignorance can have untold results. I will never again wait for the system to flush out its internal enemies; waiting for the clock to run out can indeed have devastating impact.

Someone once told me that *"When all you have is a hammer, everything looks like a nail."* There are executives who learn only one or two techniques from one or two categories. They attempt to apply them to every single problem they face for the rest of their careers. That is a problem, particularly when those models drive a company and its brands toward price and quality mediocrity.

MEDIOCRE ADVICE MAKES US MEDIOCRE

Nothing can send you toward mediocrity (and potential disaster) faster than listening to people who haven't the expertise or aren't close enough to the situation to provide truly beneficial advice. This is particularly uncomfortable when those dispensing the advice are in a position of power. They are not close enough to a situation to provide the best direction, but they think they know best anyway. It is like implementing battle plans drawn up by Knights who do not know the terrain of the kingdom they seek to defend. Here is one marketer's tale.

Anonymous Storyteller
While developing launch advertising in a major foreign market for a global food brand, our team learned from a series of in-depth

focus groups that the most promising positioning strategy would be to create a sophisticated and intensely sensual brand identity (this is what the consumers wanted). We were after the hearts and minds of this market's critical, youthful, opinion-leading segment. Succeeding with those trendsetters would lead to the pot of gold—the suburban middle class. The research results were indisputable. The young, trend-setting crowd, both men and women, would overwhelmingly respond to our message. The potential for us to OWN this identity was tremendous (all other competitors had staked out all-family positions for decades—no chance for them to consider this brand image), and the international caché of our brand gave consumers every reason to believe our message. Our team (made up entirely of experienced local marketers and yours truly, the only expatriate) and our agency were very excited.

Consistent with the style of communications in some overseas markets, our print and TV campaigns involved sexy, beautiful people playfully interacting (no clothes off—really!) with each other and the product. The message was clear: for discerning consumers, this brand delivered sophistication and sensual pleasure like no other. The campaigns were to be produced with the most highly regarded photographers and TV directors from that country.

So this sounds like marketing utopia, right? Yes, except for the dreaded international advertising approval process. This is the process where the corporate suits back at headquarters begin to dissect the communication frame by frame and want to know the following:

Exactly what comment in the focus group resulted in so many people of color appearing in this spot!

Why does that young actor need to caress the girl's thigh like that in frame #152?

Why can't you show the product with more appetite appeal?

Are you sure the lady should say that word at the end—that would be vulgar in English!

We need to run this by the other regional markets to see what changes will suit their consumers.

You get the idea.

After countless teleconferences with HQ along the lines of the above mentioned comments, and the multitude of "suggestions" that would inevitably have added months (and a lot of dollars) to create animatics, qualitatively test the concept, quantitatively test the copy, reconsider the media schedule, reconsider the programming, and ultimately seek to eliminate every iota of risk from this advertising project, we did what so many international marketing teams dream of doing—we stopped talking to headquarters. We returned very few calls from our HQ colleagues related to the project and challenged the rules instructing the international teams on how to develop advertising. Contrary to convention we didn't pursue quantitative copy testing (we trusted our judgment), we didn't breathe down the photographer's and director's necks (we didn't even send anyone to the shoot), and once aligned on a great broadcast buy we didn't second-guess the agency's media and programming recommendations. After a reasonable amount of challenge and pushback, we trusted the expertise of our carefully selected partners and we trusted our own insight and understanding of the local consumer.

The campaign is recognized (to this day, I think) for having received the most advertising awards in this market for a single season. The results for the brand were great. Follow-up image testing with the youth crowd showed the desired personality was quickly taking shape and yes, Moms thought it was cool too. The business results were terrific and sales quickly shot to the top tier of all international markets for this brand.

Moral(s) of the story:

Is anarchy (i.e. "no rules") the best way to develop communications? No, but you must try to move faster to market in developing products and communication. Reconsider all the rules being applied to teams outside HQ. Can some be eliminated to foster greater entrepreneurial efforts?

Is that entire HQ and regional staff (supporting the field) worthless? Of course not. But the better question is this: if you take great care in selecting (and highly compensating) Field Personnel, are you giving them the autonomy to deliver? If the organization is overly con-

trolling it will drive away its best performers and be left with people whose strongest skill is following procedures.

Those closest to the consumer are often best suited to identify insights. Hire the very best people; then follow them.

Don't assess all creative from your own values/aesthetic sensibilities. Understand the target.

I do not typically advise reducing communications with the corporate office as this storyteller did, but I certainly understand the predicament he was in. The Knights in the region must be the ones in charge of defending their kingdom.

HOLDING ON TO OLD WAYS MAKES US MEDIOCRE

Even if a company was glorious once upon a time, it does not mean it will stay glorious forever. Visionaries die, or leave, or have their limits. Caretakers take over, and time washes away the luster of innovation and superiority. Our once-vital companies become mediocre and stagnant.

Anonymous Storyteller
Moses and Joshua—or know your limits

Many people are good for a company (like Moses was for the Israelites), but at some point, they hit their limit. It is good when your chairman is divine and can tell Moses it is time to retire and let Joshua take over from here. Most of the time, though, people with triumphs in their past get kept in office even when their decisions start hurting, rather than helping their companies.

I was at a toy company in the mid 1990s, led by a strong, insightful leader. He was the second generation in his family to run the company, and in his time he grew the company from a "below the radar" niche player to a strong second tier company. His smarts, stubbornness, and strong belief in his vision vs. input from others served him well for many years. As he got older and as the company started fighting against a higher caliber of competition, these traits started working against him.

He believed that cable TV was an "inferior medium" and he insisted on doing most of his advertising in prime time, while the com-

petition was buying more reach and frequency with the same dollars. Despite the fact that old colleagues, who were adequate in "the old days," were losing money in their portions of the business, he did not replace them with more professional management. Despite a series of advisors, who warned of the consequences of these policies, he held course.

So the inevitable happened. His public company's stock plunged, in an otherwise robust stock market, and the company was bought by a competitor. The good news for him was that he had plenty of stock and walked away with a "set for life" payday. The bad news for him was that he could have been a lot wealthier if he could have risen to the next level. The bad news for everyone else was that if the board had really done its job, they would have intervened before it was too late. Then, the company that his family had run for decades would not have become part of the ghosts of Christmas past and hundreds of employees would not have been thrown out of work.

In the classic book, *In Search of Excellence*, authors Tom Peters and Robert Waterman Jr., state that excellent companies have "a bias for action." They go on to say that even though excellent companies "may be analytical in their approach to decision making, they are not paralyzed by that fact (as so many others seem to be)."

MEDIOCRE INDUSTRIES

The birth of entire industries is often due to one person who had a vision, and then multitudes of others followed in his or her footsteps. Think Henry Ford. Think Thomas Edison. Think Walt Disney. After a time, industries slow, the original visionary disappears, and the industry falls into doldrums. Many times the very dynamics of the industry changes, which requires another visionary to invent new ways of doing business. But if a new visionary does not arrive, the industry will do what it did in the past using old business models that are no longer good enough for today's world. The lack of vision drives them toward mediocrity and even the brink of obsolescence. Do you work at the post office, at a railroad, at a publishing company, or at a heathcare-related company? Some industries have not been able to reinvent themselves, and so they must wait for a savior that can show the way. Other industries make tragic mistakes that wound them for decades.

The advertising industry is one of these, and I think the lesson of this industry has applications to others. Here, well-intentioned Monarchs and Knights simply blew it (I think) by making decisions over many decades that resulted in mediocrity for the industry at large. I say that with great pain, as I was part of the advertising industry, and still am to some extent as part of my consulting practice.

There was a time in the 1950s, 1960s, 1970s and even the early 1980s when Madison Avenue reigned. True Monarch Visionaries helped create and shape the advertising industry during the early years. People like Bill Bernbach and David Ogilvy were significant forces. Big advertising ideas supported by big budgets were the coin of the realm. Advertising agencies were also intellectual powerhouses. They hired the best and the brightest Knights and paid them very well. They had vast research departments that dissected the dynamics of their clients' industries, probed the inner reaches of consumer psyches, and used the knowledge not just to develop great advertising, but also to help clients on an array of initiatives such as new products. Information is power and advertising agencies had it. In fact, there was even a time when clients had little or no research at all, making agencies quite valuable.

Then the power began to trickle away.

In his 1991 book *Whatever Happened to Madison Avenue?* Martin Mayer pointed out: "Through the decade of the 1980s, the relative importance of advertising to American industry steadily declined as expenditures on other sales techniques steadily increased." Whereas in 1980, he noted, advertising accounted for about two-thirds of all marketing expenditures, this decreased to about one-third by 1990 (where it remains to this day). As marketing dollars continued to go elsewhere, advertising as a central force eroded. Manufacturers began to divert more dollars to trade and consumer promotions, for example, to satisfy increasingly powerful retailers, as well as to get a short-term boost in sales.

As clients began to throw marketing dollars elsewhere (e.g. public relations, promotions, etc.), some agency Monarchs began to offer some of these services to capture a portion of those dollars. That was smart. Young & Rubicam called their approach "The Whole Egg." Ogilvy called it "Orchestration." The concept had merit. Having one company develop a brilliant brand idea and then orchestrate it across an array of communication disciplines, appeared powerful. It ensured that the brand idea is accurately upheld everywhere. It promised none of the miscues that can happen when various communications companies are involved. It promised efficiencies to a client who would deal with only one communications company and not many separate companies.

However, the agencies' own internal structures and fiefdoms sometimes got in the way. Because each subsidiary or division often had its own profit center, each would sometimes fight over who "owned" the client relationship, and which division got what piece of the pie (I remember those days too well). The divisions may have been under one roof, but they often acted as separate companies would. The potential benefits to clients were often lost. Therefore, clients would cherry pick the services they wanted. The benefits of one-stop communications were not clear.

To make matters worse, the agencies' intellectual power base declined in two key ways.

First, clients began to hire the best and the brightest and to pay them well. Level for level, agency salaries often fell below their client counterparts. Economics 101 will tell you that the best people usually go where they can make the most money (not always, but often). "A lot of clients trusted agencies to look after their affairs," said William Phillips, the retired CEO of The Ogilvy Group (quoted in *Whatever Happened to Madison Avenue?*). "Then clients became more marketing oriented and hired better marketing people themselves."

Second, clients began to staff up their research departments in order to gain control over industry and consumer knowledge. At the same time, agencies began to dismantle their research groups and so more power shifted away from the agencies. Mayer pointed out, "The division of the agency that was truly decimated in the 1980s was research." And this was not just the advertising-related research agencies gave up, but research that was used to help a client forecast the future or to aid new product development. These services helped an agency be perceived as a full business partner, but this power base fell apart.

This was exacerbated when British account planning came to America. At its most rudimentary, account planning is simply a philosophy and a practice that an agency uses to gain insights about a consumer, to beneficially position a brand in the consumer's life. In fact, account planning was used in America for quite some time before the British invasion of the 1980s, although many planners would have you think otherwise. Regardless, to sell the *concept* of planning to clients in America in the 1980s and 1990s, some planning agencies attacked other agencies' research base. "*Researchers*," a planning agency might say, "simply give you only facts and figures, whereas *account planners* give you insights into the consumer's relationship with the brand." Hence, *researchers* are bad and *planners* are good. It was the same tactic that Scope used to reposition Listerine ("medicine breath").

Many agency heads dismantled what was left of their research departments and brought in planners (sometimes they just changed their titles). Many good researchers, confounded by the situation, left the agency business, leaving a void of people who were good at research used in ways that went well beyond advertising. Frankly many planners relied too much on qualitative research at a time when client researchers became far more quantitatively oriented.

While planning was hailed as the next big thing by agencies in the 1980s, its arrival eventually helped make agencies collectively weaker by undermining an already-declining research and knowledge base at a time when clients' research, knowledge, and quantitative skills were dramatically increasing. The balance of power had shifted. Around that same time, the holding companies (Massive Kingdoms) began to rise. Companies such as the WPP Group began a buying and consolidation frenzy that included advertising agencies, public relations companies, research companies, and so forth. Their aim was to provide communication and marketing services to clients on a massive scale. Advertising agencies were gobbled up and many kicked themselves for going public in the first place, which some believe also contributed to their decline. The holding companies sometimes spun off the other communication and marketing companies those agencies had acquired, leaving the agency looking like it had decades earlier. More recently, some agencies were stripped of their media departments as well, which were also spun off as separate entities. That has left some agencies looking like extremely large creative boutiques because the essential remaining departments are creative, account service, and sometimes account planning.

Net: Advertising agencies, once a true power on Madison Avenue and in control of the majority of marketing and media dollars, have become small brands in someone else's portfolio. In fact, one source estimated that advertising now brings in less than half of these holding companies' revenue. The holding companies function like packaged goods manufacturers' approach to controlling shelf space. The more brands you have on the shelf, the more likely that a client will buy one of yours. Want to fire Ogilvy? That's okay. You can buy from one of our other advertising agencies like JWT or Y&R. Want more PR and less advertising? That's okay because we have that, too. Will the holding companies be able to orchestrate all of their companies to provide a seamless offering to clients from advertising to public relations to research and more? That is hard to imagine, particularly since each unit within these holding companies has its own profit center to worry about. That means turf wars.

Agencies bemoan the situation they helped to create. One agency CEO recently told a gathering of industry nobility that respect for the industry is dwindling. Duh! When all agencies look alike, and provide fewer and fewer services, at a time when clients are demanding more, respect is hard earned. "Our day is coming," said this same agency head. Not likely, for agencies have all but ignored other storms on the horizon. And those storms could very well bury them. More and more consumer eyeballs are turning toward the internet. One recent study showed that the amount of time people spend on the internet jumped to 10 to 15 percent of their total media time. Yet media spending on this platform is only about 2.5 percent. Most advertising agencies, still accustomed to old media and unable to "break the code" of grabbing a consumer's attention on the internet, are about to take another fall, particularly since new technologies allow consumers to bypass traditional television advertising altogether. Studies show that as many as

71 percent of those who use DVRs (Digital Video Recorders) bypass the ads. New versions of DVRs allow consumers to skip the ads with the push of a button, without fast-forwarding.

Yes, agencies have to deliver big creative ideas (though many accuse them of creating art as opposed to selling products). Yes, agencies have to understand the consumers and use the knowledge to build and maintain brands. This idea has been around for a couple of decades, but that is where the agency business began even before the heyday of Madison Avenue. So what's next?

No one knows. While great talent has emerged occasionally to shake up the industry with great advertising (e.g. Jay Chiat, Hal Riney), there is no one on the horizon who can truly reinvent the way advertising agencies do business—at least not that I can see. Yet some of the best and the brightest Knights I know remain in advertising, and I have had the good fortune to work with some of them to this very day. They have stuck it out, mostly out of the love for what they do. Their clients also need them desperately. However, the industry, by and large, has failed them over many years by making collectively poor decisions.

By now, those readers who are not connected to the advertising business are probably nodding off. However, please pay close attention for just one more moment, because what happened to the advertising business can happen anywhere. The drive toward mediocrity that enveloped the entire industry was a result of the following five simple but powerful factors:

Underpaying human resources that resulted in shrinking the available pool of the best and the brightest;

Destroying a powerful knowledge and research base which provided value to clients (information is power);

Failing to restructure a business internally in order to better meet client needs;

An inability to get ahead of the curve of key consumer trends; and

The absence of a visionary messiah who can show the entire industry the way to rejuvenate itself.

REINVENTION HELPS KILL MEDIOCRITY

Peter Drucker stated that while "core competencies are different for every organization . . . every organization needs one core competence: innovation."

No debate. Yet I think here, too, we deceive ourselves (truly as the namesakes of Don Quixote). The respondents in our Survey of 100 virtually all believe that their company is a recognized innovator in its industry. Can't be; at least not in a way that consumers will be able to discern. But it's better for our egos, I suppose, that we believe it's true.

⬛ SURVEY OF 100

Sixty-six percent agreed completely that their company is a recognized innovator in its industry; 20 percent agreed somewhat; 11 percent disagreed. Interestingly, however, 47 percent also agreed (completely or somewhat) that their company asks for new ideas, but does not always have the courage to use them.

The problem is that if we believe it's true that each of our companies are innovators, then we rest assured that everything is A-OK, and we stop pushing the limits. *It's better that we always believe ourselves to be lagging behind, for that is the only way to ensure we will innovate.* This is a corollary to my advice that it is always better to assume we are incompetent, which will force us towards competence.

To slay mediocrity, kingdoms and Knights must embrace reinvention. This applies not only to massive reinvention of industries, but for small everyday reinventions as well. It is scary, and few have the constitution for it, but it is vital. Some reinvention happens through baby steps and some through massive overhauls to address fundamental shifts in marketplace and consumer needs.

Witness Betty Crocker. One of my best recollections of my time at General Mills was that of a hallway where portraits of Betty Crocker were hung. Though a fictitious character, she has been one of the most recognized figures in packaged goods for decades. As you stepped along the hallway, from the beginnings of her reign to modern day, Betty

Crocker does not age. Instead, each portrait grows younger with each new decade, to reflect the more youthful demographics of the day. It was my first small lesson about reinventing one's company and brands for the times.

Witness Madonna. Every few years, she reinvents her persona, look, and music in order to not just reflect the times, but to create the trends and fads that others will follow. She is a trailblazer.

Witness Microsoft. If there were ever a company that was manic in its drive to cover all bets in all types of innovation, this one is it. Having a finger in everything is a good way to ensure that you aren't left behind (that is, if you can afford to have a finger in everything).

Witness the toy industry, a fad business, one in which kids do not want yesterday's toys, they want what is new today. Astute toy makers have learned to re-invent their brands year after year to reflect the times and to convey a sense of "newness." One of the best examples, mentioned in an earlier chapter, is Barbie. When little girls wanted to be a fashion model, Barbie was a fashion model. When little girls wanted to be a nurse, she became a nurse. When little girls were beginning to feel more empowered, Barbie became an astronaut and more. Barbie not only reflected girls' desires, but led them as well.

Witness MTV. At its inception, it created a forum in which upcoming artists would get exposure through music videos, and in so doing, the artists' contemporary styles would rub off on MTV itself. Because it needs to stay contemporary, MTV is forced to stay in touch with its audience, thus fostering continuous renewal.

No organization is exempt. The dynasties in Europe eventually fell in part because they could not adjust to society's shifting circumstances and needs. In contrast, it is interesting to note that the founding fathers of the United States Constitution allowed for *amendments* to the constitution. They realized that times change, and that the government needed a process in which the people's voices, heard through a representative form of government, could change the very nature of the Constitution itself. Hence, the Constitution satisfies timeless human needs, in ways that can adjust with the times. It can renew itself. The framers of the Constitution were visionaries. Mediocre they were not.

A Knight's Code of Business

Sustained Superiority: A Good Knight seeks sustained superiority through excellence, which can only come through sustained effort and periodic reinvention.

And Other Advice

Good Knights, refuse to settle for sameness, though there are great and mighty forces that will entreat you. Cultivate a bias for action, and never assume that you are innovative *enough*. Apply the right business models to the right circumstances.

Good Squires-in-Training, be relentless in your drive to make the projects within your care superior and innovative, and you will soon be knighted. If your boss is mediocre, find a new boss. If your company is mediocre, find a new company. If your industry is mediocre throughout, consider finding a new industry. Unless you are the true messiah who can turn an entire industry about, your career will languish.

Good Monarchs, take a hard, objective look at your kingdom and your industry. Compare it to where it was in the glory days. If these are the glory days, you are blessed. If they are not, find and unleash a visionary who will turn your company on its head. (That visionary may be right under your nose.) Never let your kingdom's core strengths be taken from you by either competitors or your own clients. Do not be afraid to restructure your company to better embrace new business realities, and stay ahead of the curve in consumer trends. You will discover that when word spreads that your kingdom is known for unflinching superiority and innovation, customers and clients will seek you out, and other great artisans and craftsmen will want to live in your kingdom, bringing with them the best skills and wares, which will forever perpetuate superiority and kill mediocrity.

Chapter 13

Tomfoolery
(Style Overwhelming Substance)

"Sancho. Sancho. There are times for joking and times when jokes are out of place."

—DON QUIXOTE

With such a vast array of colorful characters that dwell within the kingdom, there are apt to be plentiful stories about the silly things that they sometimes do. We are not disappointed, for we all do silly things. Serfs do silly things, as do Knights and Monarchs and Barons and so on. It happens with some frequency, notably because we are human. This you know firsthand. It is all a form of tomfoolery.

There's one particular aspect of tomfoolery that is worth addressing in a business context because it warrants caution: when style overwhelms substance, beware. This type of tomfoolery can hide deeper truths. Some executives routinely emphasize sizzling style over straightforward content because content is lacking, and so they try to dazzle their audience with meaningless theatrics to appear bigger and better than they are. Other times style simply backfires. On other occasions, some executives cannot tell the difference between style and substance. They genuinely think style is substance. That is the greatest danger, though any time style overwhelms substance and content, it sets the stage for incompetence and poor decision-making.

 **SURVEY OF 100**

> Twelve percent agreed (completely or somewhat) that many top executives in their companies put too much emphasis on style instead of substance.

This is not to say that style is bad. It is not at all. Style can help sell points of view, divisions, and entire businesses, but it becomes dangerous when people mistake one for the other. To use a cliché, they buy the sizzle and ignore the quality of the steak. It is silly, but we are drawn into it. Think internet start-ups. An entire industry came from nowhere, soared, and went bust in the short-term. That is because we were caught up in the hype, in the style, in the excitement, and didn't take the time to dig into the content. This was nothing short of mass Tomfoolery. How did we not know better than to be sucked into the silliness of it?

This chapter could have easily been an overview of the internet start-up boom-to-bust saga, but you've already heard it, lived it, and probably lost money due to it. Instead, most of the following are tales of what happens when advertising agencies pitch new business. Agencies, in their maddening drive to capture business and to differentiate themselves in an industry driven toward mediocrity, have done all sorts of dumb things (I'm guilty in this). There is no better place to find examples of misguided style overwhelming content. Moreover, the stories are probably sillier than anything you might read about internet start-ups. Wait, I could be wrong, but let me proceed anyway.

Let's begin with several rather silly stories that reveal misguided style, and we will move to more serious examples later.

EGG ON YOUR FACE

The advertising agency I once worked for got a call from an Egg Commission, a noble marketing organization whose objective is to promote the consumption of eggs. They wanted a new advertising agency and invited several to pitch their business. Our agency arrived at the first meeting to meet the prospective client, do pleasantries, and get a briefing by the client on their business objectives and situation. During a coffee break, as I was chatting with the chief client, he confided in me that he was initially not sure whether he should invite our agency to pitch his business because of our behavior the last time we pitched him. Having not been involved with the pitch some years earlier, but knowing the management that was, I was suddenly intrigued as to what they might have done to have turned this rather likable guy against them. So I asked.

"You can't imagine what they did," he began as I recall. "To get my attention during the pitch process, they sent a live chicken—I said a *live* chicken—to my office on a Friday afternoon with a note about your agency's capabilities." He paused, then continued with a befuddled look on his face. "What in heaven do you do with a *live* chicken on a Friday afternoon? Can't bring it home. Can't leave it at the office because it could die over the weekend. What, exactly, were they thinking?"

Style sabotaged the content of the message the agency was trying to impart, whatever that was.

A DOG'S LIFE

Years later, I helped an advertising agency win a computer hardware account. After the pitch, I asked the client what we did right, and what the other agencies did wrong. It always helps for the next pitch. With a sudden look of disdain on our new client's face, she began to tell me that another agency, to make some point, brought a caged dog into the presentation room. Apparently, the dog looked rather afraid to be in this setting, making the agency people look like arrogant bullies. Whatever point that agency was trying to make was lost. The clients only felt appalled that the agency executives would be so heartless. It didn't help that the clients were all dog lovers.

Again, style devoured content.

HIGH-TECH THEATRICS: STYLE OR SUBSTANCE?

We once pitched an advertising assignment for a new cable channel, whose point of difference (or so they told us) was an abundance of live programming. Live programming means that they would have to move fast and furiously day in and day out. The pitch process reflected this fast pace as well. The new channel had to make an immediate decision as to which agency to hire, then an immediate decision as to what positioning strategy to take. Thus, the agencies were given a miniscule amount of time to mount a full strategic and creative exploratory, and no time at all to research it before presenting it to the prospective client.

We wanted to demonstrate that we, as an agency, could move as fast and as furiously as our prospective client. My boss at the time, Jerry McGee who ran Ogilvy LA, came up with one of the most innovative pitch theatrics we ever implemented. It was style and sizzle, yet it had a point: our ability to move fast!

The idea, which was orchestrated in only a couple of days, was this: A focus group would be conducted live, and broadcast back to the client's offices, during the pitch, in real time. Here is how it worked. After Jerry presented the overview to the client, he tossed the pitch to me. I presented our strategic insights about their business and then the positioning recommendation. As the creative team began to present its recommended advertising (three different campaign ideas), I quietly slipped out the back door and raced to the agency about five miles away where we had assembled the focus group of about 10 consumers. As I entered the room, technicians wired me for sound, checked and rechecked the audio and visual feed that would bounce off a satellite that was miles above the Earth, and down into the presentation room, unbeknownst to the clients in the room. It was touch and go, as we had been gaining and losing the satellite link all morning, but for the moment anyway, we had it. After the creative team delivered its work, Jerry rose to address the clients once more. He said that given the tight timetable, there was not enough time to conduct research either before or after the presentation. So we decided to do it today, live, reflecting the nature of the channel that the client was creating, and demonstrating that our agency was capable of moving fast. He then moved to a full, floor-to-ceiling cabinet at the head of the room, took a breath, and opened it, praying that on the television screen before him he would see me, staring back at him. He was not disappointed. I was on the screen. However, did we have sound?

"Gene, can you hear me?" he asked, apprehensively.

"Yes, loud and clear!" I said.

The clients were amazed, looking to the back of the room for me, smiling when they realized that I had slipped out. We then proceeded with the focus group by exposing the consumers to our strategy and our three advertising options as the clients watched on their television monitor. The consumers actually loved our strategy, and of the three campaigns we showed them, they loved one, hated one, and were neutral about the third.

It was a gutsy, innovative thing to do. It could have been a disaster. The satellite link might have been lost. The consumers may have hated our strategy and all the work.

However, we did not get the business. I never knew why. Was this simply tomfoolery, and the client thought us to be too clever by half? Maybe. At least this tomfoolery had a point, or so we thought. Style isn't bad per se, unless it doesn't support content, or if the resources devoted to it drain time from other efforts that matter more.

THE STYLE AND EGO THAT CONSUMES

We now move to the type of tomfoolery that has more dire consequences, because it comes wrapped in charisma and ego and force of will. Even the best management can be fooled, for some people can exude so much of it, they appear to know what they are doing when they do not. Politics is filled with such characters, and as it happens, so is business.

Anonymous Storyteller

A fast-track manager at an oral-care company I used to work for was moved from sales to marketing to help round out his skills. In his first position as a marketing product manager he was given the most generic of our products—dental floss. With determination to succeed and a gift for gab, he convinced higher ups throughout the company that with a slight variation on our current floss we would see vastly greater consumer acceptance. Based on his sheer force of will, huge share gains were projected for this "new" floss and production was ramped up drastically. After the launch of the product, he was promoted for handling the entire launch so well. Of course, the launch of a new product and its success are two different things. Since dental floss isn't really a "high involvement" product, getting consumers to pay a premium for this "new" floss was a tough sell that never materialized. The product manager who took over the floss line then had the unenviable task of getting rid of warehouse after warehouse of dental floss, and got blamed for not coming close to matching the budget numbers for his product line.

The next story shows an even more devilish outcome when style, combined with a grand ego, completely overwhelms substance.

A Story by Gary Elliott

A large, successful New York company had just purchased a sleepy, one-office firm 3,000 miles away to gain a foothold in a promising western market. The local 100+ person operation was dominated by one client, which accounted for about 90 percent of its revenues. The local client was profitable and had a reputation for old time quality and values, but had a lackluster image.

A new slate of senior managers was recruited to bring some 'spark' to this client's marketing and kick-start a new-business drive. One of the starring new cast, recruited from another city, heralded himself as a creative superstar—solo inventor of three highly recognizable campaigns. In fact, they were iconic campaigns. With exceedingly handsome features, a glib Hollywood repartee and a god-like, bulletproof ego, he had an immediate effect on employees and clients. He seemed bigger than life; some wondered why he ever left the bright lights to come to the backwater.

He set about to reinvent the company, the client, and the market.

As the new office was busy reorganizing itself and weeding out "non-performers," the client wanted to know when it might begin to see the benefit of this new talent.

Our hero stepped forward to the challenge. His ideas were radical, expensive, and quite out-of-character for this client. His confidence and ego lessened the client's initial reluctance to change.

He passionately argued for his ideas. "Campaigns of the past were formulaic and boring," he said. He demanded a complete overhaul—out with the old—"if we can't get new thinking then we'll get new people." Tempers and stress-levels rose; morale, once euphoric, was now on life-support. There was room in the tent for those with his good taste only. Differing views were not solicited; you were either on the "team" or on your way out.

The client went along with several of the proposed ideas—allocating both money and resources. Before long, the marketplace confirmed that this new brand of marketing was actually hurting sales. As the first metrics came in, so did the toll on the people with whom the client had been working so closely over the years.

Things had gotten out of hand; the client petitioned the New York headquarters to fix this mess.

One fateful February morning the entire local office staff was summoned. Such a gathering did not bode well.

The superstar took front and center. "I have some good news and bad news," he said. "What would you like to hear first?"

Someone at the rear shouted, "Give us the bad news."

"Well," he said slowly, "Today, we have lost our key client. They will be moving the business to New York."

"What does this mean to the office?" the same person asked.

"Most of you will be losing your jobs."

The room groaned.

"What's the good news?"

His retort left the room speechless. "I love each and every one of you."

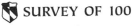 **SURVEY OF 100**

Twenty-three percent agreed (completely or somewhat) that some of their top executives got ahead on charisma instead of talent.

Do not confuse charisma and style with competence and substance. Charlatans, some aristocrats, and Evil Barons often use the former to convince the unsuspecting that they have the latter. Those that know better value humility and substance.

NOTHING BUT CONTENT

I pitched a new division of Pacific Bell years ago while at Ogilvy. We avoided anything that smacked of tomfoolery. No glitz. No glam. Nothing silly. Egos were left at home. We just pitched it with hard, nose-to-the-grindstone, honest, get-down-to-business work. During the initial capabilities pitch when we were asked to demonstrate our credentials, we decided to talk only about the client's business, and to demonstrate our credentials that way.

For the pitch, we constructed a huge decision wall as follows (okay, maybe there was a little style): The first section of the wall had alternate brand objectives the client might face (given the environment) listed in a long column. To the right of that listing was a list of alternate target audiences. To the right of that was a listing of alternate brand messages. To the right of that was a listing of alternate support points, and onward through media alternatives, promotional strategies, and so on.

During the pitch, we took the clients through each column, one at a time, from the larger strategic issues on the left toward the more tactical ones on the right. We used the wall to help us focus upon and debate alternative directions with the clients. The clients were immediately engaged because we were debating the core elements of their business. Importantly, we did not pretend to have the solution or the ultimate answer; many agencies always feel it is necessary to provide THE answer, even though they have been working on the business only two weeks. Instead, we said that we knew the answer was somewhere in those lists, and that we were willing to work with the client to discover it. We accomplished something grand. We showed our command of their issues, a willingness to work with them, and a framework for finding the right answer.

We were awarded the business the very next day. In fact, the client ended the pitch process early. Initially the client intended to take another step and ask all of the agencies that were pitching to produce creative work. However, having been exposed to our raw, uncensored, unscripted discussion, they had found something in us they liked. No glitz. No glam. No ego. No tomfoolery. Just substance.

A Knight's Code of Business

Sensibility: A Good Knight can distinguish tomfoolery from what truly matters, valuing substance above style, and placing humility before boastfulness.

And Other Advice

Good Knight, have fun with style and use it to make your point, but never be a slave to it.

Good Squires-in-Training, learn content foremost, and style secondarily. For as it happens, style can be quite useful when delivering content and making it exciting. Always know the difference between the two. Be the showman if you must, but deliver the goods.

Good Monarchs, beware of those who demonstrate an over reliance on style and sizzle, as they may lead you and your kingdom to act in incompetent ways. Charlatans and Evil Barons, in particular, use style and boldness to disguise shortcomings in content.

Evil Barons and Charlatans, the world has shifted in just the past few decades, placing greater emphasis on measurable results. An over reliance on style and bravado, as no time before, will serve to unmask you. So keep it up!

Chapter 14

Futility

"Consider what you are and try to know yourself, which is the most difficult study in the world."

—Don Quixote

Futility could be discussed only near the end of our journey through misadventures in character and competence, for futility occurs only when such negative behaviors become chronic. We might keep trying to achieve noble goals for our companies, and time and again some of us are thwarted due to the same prolonged incompetence or low moral character of those around us—and ourselves. This is disheartening for any brave Knight, in any kingdom, for constantly filling a leaky bucket with fresh water is tiring.

We begin to feel that our efforts are futile. We become disenchanted, angry, and jaded. If you have felt this way, you are in good company.

SURVEY OF 100

Nineteen percent agreed (completely or somewhat) that it is often futile to try to make a real, positive difference in their companies.

Most futility has its genesis in the same corporate and human failing; *the failure to address a fundamental issue of competence or character.* Ignoring a problem makes it grow, which impedes efforts to fix it. Futility can be overcome only by taking a good look at ourselves and our companies, identifying root problems, and then fixing them. However, many times we do not, because the problems are such a tangled mess that we prefer to ignore them. We even begin to think of our situation as "normal" because of the problem's longevity. As the problems grow and impede noble efforts, futility grows. Good Knights and Squires waste time and resources in pursuits that will never bear fruit because a fundamental problem remains unchallenged.

Thinking back to the lessons in past chapters, some common futilities are these:

- If you dwell in an entrenched aristocracy, attempts to be adequately compensated based upon merit are often futile, for a disproportionate amount of money and accolades will often stay at the top.

- If you work in environments where duplicity is left unchecked, your honest efforts will often be thwarted.

- If you work in environments where larceny is often condoned at the top, your job and retirement funds will never be fully secure.

- If you work in environments where indecency is often rampant, gossip and lawsuits may eat up time and resources.

- If you work in environments that often breed fear, you will seldom be allowed to innovate.

- If you work in environments where various maladies are often left unresolved, you will seldom have pleasant working conditions and you may actually be in harm's way.

- If you work in environments where insincerity is commonplace, you will seldom be told the truth about your shortcomings, and hence, cannot fix them.

- If you work in environments where many people are not passionate about their craft, you will seldom attain your best because you must depend upon them.

- If you work in environments where there is no visionary or vision, your company will never break through to the next level of greatness.

- If you work in environments where communication is routinely poor, you will seldom be able to work as one.
- If you work in environments where grand plans are often met with mediocre execution, you will seldom be superior.
- If you work in environments where style is often elevated over substance, you will seldom be respected for content.
- If you work in environments where many of these weaknesses in character or competence often reign, you are in a sorry state, indeed.

Know the world in which you live, and the aspects within yourself that lead to futility. Some examples:

CHRONIC FEAR OF RISK

A client once challenged our advertising agency to develop a new, breakthrough media approach for an upcoming new product launch. This is one of the same clients I spoke of earlier. The media group toiled, and toiled, and toiled some more until it had developed a magnificent media plan and implementation approach. I was invited to the presentation to lend support for the media group by answering any oddball questions that might arise.

The presentation went beautifully. Our media team presented a truly innovative plan. It included new, topnotch innovative media techniques that would touch consumers in various ways, throughout their daily lives, using methods that would break out of clutter and be truly meaningful and fun for the audience.

The client was impressed. They applauded our media group and said it was the *best* media plan they had ever seen. Ever! And it was. The entire team left the meeting truly excited, for they were about to embark on a great task, to implement all that they had recommended.

Fast-forward a few months. When the new product was actually launched, none—not ONE—of the many innovative ideas were implemented, nor even tested in market. The client did what they always had done for new product launches: run a thirty second TV commercial in prime time. Why were all of the innovative ideas rejected? The client was afraid to take a risk on something new. This was one incident among many.

After a time, the agency found it hard to mount such efforts, because so many of them were futile. It is easy for a manufacturer to ask for great thinking, but having the bravery to implement it is something else altogether. The real problem had nothing to do with a media plan. The real problem had everything to do with an organization that consistently bred an aversion to risk. It was chronic. The real problem was ignored. Years of one futile attempt to innovate after another led to a feeling of helplessness.

The same can happen at any company around the world, and in every division and every department.

CHRONIC DENIAL

One of my employees was once terribly unhappy. Who am I kidding? I've had many employees who, for one reason or another, were terribly unhappy at some point, but let me talk about one of them. Her clients were tough, her hours were long, and the work she was given was too mundane. Knowing that I had a raise coming and she did not, I went to my boss, asked that my raise be given to my employee instead, and told him that I would wait yet another year for mine. So she got the raise that was meant for me.

I know that I mentioned this glorious story in an earlier chapter. What I didn't tell you in the earlier chapter was that I was in denial. I kept ignoring the real problem. It was not about money. It was about the quality of her work environment and it was terrible. Her assignments were brutal at times. The work was truly mundane. It reeked. I let it go on because I had my hands filled with other stuff, and I did not take the time to find a solution. Instead of addressing the more difficult problem of her work environment, I tried the far easier solution of throwing money at her, even if it was my own.

It was futile. Within three months of getting a raise meant for me, my employee quit anyway (I never told her, by the way, that she got my raise). It was completely, and utterly, my fault. I had ignored the real issue. Not only was I out an employee, but I was out a raise as well. I still had to wait a year for another.

Could I have addressed her problems? Yes, I think so. However, it would have required moving people around and thinking up new projects to intrigue her. That is what I should have done, but I was in chronic denial. I learned the hard way, because I eventually had to expend a lot of time anyway in order to find and train her replacement.

CHRONIC ARISTOCRACIES

Some aristocrats try too hard to fit in with other aristocrats, and it can become a chronic lifestyle that affects nearly everything.

I'm going to tell you a secondhand story. I need to warn you of this because while I asked all of the story contributors to provide only first-hand accounts, this one is secondhand. I was one of those secondhand parties, as were several others. I called the others involved, and they provided slightly different accounts of the story. I'll share the aspects of the story that are in common. If this story is true (and I believe it is), it sheds small but added light on troublesome and nebulous issues.

A very long time ago we developed advertising for a client. We tested the advertising among consumers before we ran it, and it tested very well. In fact, it was among the top performing pieces of advertising this client had ever tested. It was very competitive and made a good case why people should buy my client's products over competitive products.

But wait. The advertising ran only once. That's right. It ran only once! Then the marketing client called and told us to stop running the ad. This startled us, as we had put a lot of time and effort into a great piece of advertising that showed promise of truly helping the sales of this client's products.

"Why must we pull our ad?" we asked the marketing client.

Here's what we were told. Our client's chairman ran into another chairman of a competitive company at the club (or golf course or fundraiser, etc.). The other chairman, our competitor, said some disparaging things about the ad. Our client's chairman then decided he did not like it either, and told his marketing staff to pull it. This was despite the fact that the ad was tested and scored very well with consumers, and was very competitive at that!

This is what is called the old boy's network. It raises an interesting issue. It says that while *some* aristocrats rule their kingdoms, they also can be heavily influenced by aristocrats that rule other kingdoms. It says there's an inner circle at the very top, and those who fly within it have far more in common with each other than they do with those in their own kingdoms. It also says that, on occasion, a Monarch *might* ignore what is best for his or her company in order to stroke his or her ego among the corporate elite.

That brings chronic futility for all those down below. We are told to compete with competitors. But how can that be achieved in situations when some Monarchs consort with the enemy, finding more in common with those at the top of other realms than with those within their own kingdom.

However, that was long ago in a kingdom whose players are long gone. You decide how far fetched it really is, and whether it is possible that such antics still operate today, here and there, now and then, by a few, in castles far above the clouds where no one can see. Think mega-mergers. Do they all really happen for the benefit of the corporations, or do *some* fuel the egos of the Monarchs who, as it happens, see each other with some frequency? This clubby association is in full swing among some supposed independent directors on boards. It doesn't help that CEOs are commonly on each other's boards. *Fortune* magazine interviewed a board member [guaranteeing anonymity] to better understand what happens when executive compensation is debated. The board member confided, "Basically, what people understand they have to do is go along with management, because if they don't they won't be a part of the club." So much for independence.

Chronic aristocracies cannot achieve their best, because they are chronic aristocracies.

CHRONIC TRADITIONS

The Roman Catholic Church does not like change. In fact, most of the other Christian faiths only came about because the Roman Catholic Church did not adapt fast enough to the prevailing attitudes, and so the church splintered many times over. As you also know, the Catholic Church is attempting to stop sexual abuse of its parishioners perpetrated by *some* deviant priests. Though the church has been slow to acknowledge the situation and slow to react, it has finally and publicly denounced the inappropriate actions by various priests, and has also assembled codes of conduct.

However, these changes may prove futile because the church is chronically following the tradition of celibacy, which may be the fundamental issue. Priests are not allowed to marry, due to orders dating back hundreds of years. The decision in favor of celibacy was made, in part, because the church wanted to inherit the possessions of priests when they died, and did not want to lose those possessions to a priest's family. Celibacy may inadvertently result in two behaviors. First, it creates normal sexual tension in normal priests. Many are forced to seek an outlet. One expert who conducted a 25-year study of celibacy, reported *Newsweek*, claimed that 50 percent of priests are sexually active in some way. More important, I think, is that the tradition of celibacy may inadvertently encourage not-so-normal priests to join the priesthood. Hence, the church may recruit not only devoted, healthy celibates, but also more than its fair share of sexually dysfunctional individuals. It is a matter of probability (and I realize some conjecture), but if you set criteria that are not in keeping with what we might consider to be normal behavior, don't you invite more not-so-normal behaviors?

As long as the church follows chronic tradition, it will invite chronic behaviors. Allowing priests to marry will not resolve all the issues, to be sure, but it would more than likely reduce the depth of the problem. The Catholic Church prefers to downplay this issue, and so, its attempt to weed out misfits may prove futile because of an age-old policy that may actually encourage them.

TOO BROKEN FOR SMALL FIXES, TOO POLITICALLY CHARGED TO REINVENT

Our newspapers are filled with stories about businesses that struggle in great, futile attempts to fix their problems, in ways that have nothing to do with the real issues at hand. In some cases, that is because the situation is too broken for quick fixes, but too politically charged to be reinvented, which is what is really needed.

There is a shortage of nurses everywhere. Hospitals try what they can to entice nurses, which includes recruiting them from far away places, giving them signing bonuses, and trying to provide more flexible hours (to an extent). None of these strategies really works in the long term. Here's the proof: the American Hospital Association claims that more than 125,000 nurses are needed across the nation. The number of nurses younger than age 30, reported the *Los Angeles Times* in 2002, has dropped 41 percent since 1983. Overall, the nurse population is aging, because too few new ones are joining the profession.

The problem is basic. There are too few nurses because they are not paid well enough for what they must do. This has also had an impact on nursing education, for there are too few instructors. Why? Because they can make more money elsewhere! A signing bonus helps once, but nurses need to survive day-to-day over a career spanning decades. Pay them a better wage, and you will have more nurses flooding into nursing schools, and more instructors waiting to teach them.

However, the money is not there. Hospitals won't pay better salaries. Insurance companies squeeze them. Yet, the heads of these insurance companies often make millions. Do I smell an entrenched and entitled Aristocracy at work? The problem is the whole healthcare system, not a "shortage of nurses." The system is broken. Attempts to create more nurses are futile. We need to reinvent healthcare. But that's a political nightmare involving a web of politicians and special interests, a mix of both Good Knights and Evil Barons, at the highest levels of business and government.

We will not have enough nurses. They will not be paid what they are worth (meritocracy). Patients will suffer. It is futile. The same applies to a vast array of industries in which noble yet futile efforts are made from below, in endeavors that cannot be fixed unless radical change comes from on high.

CHRONIC INDECISION

There are people put in positions of authority who are racked with chronic indecision. Anyone who must work with them is destined to live an anguished, futile life. Here's a story. I do not know if this particular person was chronically indecisive, but I have known others who fit this description perfectly.

Anonymous Storyteller

A number of years ago, our advertising agency pitched a large account. It was a big pitch, with the chairman of each company, and about 12 people from each company. The advertising team went to the pitch site the night before to get organized. Late that night, the agency's creative director decided that he did not like the creative pitch, and spent the entire night, all alone, rewriting the creative part of the presentation, by hand, on the back of the presentation boards. He told no one of the changes.

So instead of presenting the beautiful boards his creative and production teams had spent weeks carefully crafting, he presented his hand-written scrawls. No one could read what he had written.

The creative director started by saying he had three campaigns, but the first two he was going to present were not very good. Then he spent a half-hour presenting two campaigns for which he clearly had little heart. His last campaign, the "good one," was something about a gold standard. It raised a question from the chairman that referring to gold might not help with current market perception that the company was expensive versus the competition. The creative director thought for a minute, said it was a very perceptive question, and he would have to get back to him on it.

The chairman then left the room, even though there was still about one-third of the agency presentation to go. After the meeting, the creative director felt that his leaving meant that we had already sold him and he did not need to see anything else. He was really happy with the way things went. We did not win the pitch, and the CD left the agency two weeks later.

And another story of indecision.

Anonymous Storyteller

Big company loves us. Wants us to be their agency because we have offices in NY and LA. We are the odds-on fave. "We're looking at other agencies but that's just a formality. Can't wait! See you."

During the pitch prep, a difference of opinion arises between the media folk of NY and LA. About strategy. It begins on the phone, continues into the joint meeting the night before the pitch in LA.

The pitch next day: No settlement of this disagreement but a senior account person decides to let the client in on it "so they can be part of the process." Hey, great idea!
We never saw them again.

All the effort of so many was futile because of indecision. Do you know of a situation like that?

Today's businesses need executives who can recognize the true barriers toward achieving greatness, and then smash them. This is the ultimate effectiveness. Without such abilities, the kingdom is ineffectual, and efforts are futile.

A Knight's Code of Business

Effectual: A Good Knight forces the kingdom to address the real problems, no matter how difficult the task, for that is the only way to slay futility.

And Other Advice

Good Knights, be wary of those endeavors in which noble attempts meet continued resistance. Chances are there is a fundamental issue not being addressed. Seek the true cause of the resistance, and smash through it.

Good Squires-in-Training, if you live in a kingdom that perpetuates one futile effort after another, try what you can, but realize that some kingdoms prefer futility, and if you decide that yours is one of those, leave for a new kingdom.

Good Monarchs, allow your people to smash the barriers that lead to futility. However, if you haven't the disposition to let them do so, at the very least do not ask for great efforts when you haven't the will to act upon them. That does more damage than not asking for great work in the first place.

End Game

Chapter 15

A Knight's Code of Business

"If you follow these precepts, Sancho, your days will be long and your renown eternal, your rewards will be without number and your happiness unimaginable."

—Don Quixote

We live in a cynical world. The reputations of age-old institutions we once revered have been torn down, or at least, have been badly tarnished. It was not the institutions that were at fault, however, but the people that dwelled within them that did not meet our collective expectations. These expectations can be harsh and hypocritical. We demand perfection in others, yet we make allowances for our own flaws. We are eager to reveal human failings in others, but we are equally quick to hide our own. This dichotomy has made us weak.

Transform yourself, first, and you will begin to transform the institution you work within and the other institutions around you. Behave in accordance with higher principles, and those around you will seek a higher standard to match your own. I have witnessed this first hand, and have been terribly grateful to know true Good Knights whose standards made me better.

Because we live in a cynical world, talk of achieving high ideals is often thought to be naïve and corny. I wish to believe otherwise. I wish to believe in ideals that may seem beyond our reach at times, but are obtainable through diligence. I wish to believe that honor does exist, as does truthfulness and fairness. However, it takes a brave heart to follow such precepts consistently, because there are tremendous forces at work, both within us and from the outside, that strive to make us do otherwise.

When boiled down to the core, and all the sentiment is cleared away, character and competence are about a simple attitude that affects an array of behaviors. Though simple, it can be very difficult to implement day after day. But it gets easier with each challenge accomplished.

Following a set of principles is not easy. I have worked in or around the advertising industry for over 20 years. It is not an industry that is thought to be highly principled (yet you might be surprised that overall, it is). One study conducted some years ago asked people to rank dozens of professions by honesty and integrity. They "graded" advertising executives a "C" on these measures, far below fireman and teachers, though slightly above cab drivers, U.S. Senators, lawyers, Wall Street executives, and congressmen (in that order). Yet, I have never been in an advertising meeting where someone inferred or implied, "Hey, let's put one over on the American people." There are many market forces that prevent dishonesty: Consumers may stop buying your product,;consumer groups will protest; government agencies will investigate and prosecute infractions; and of course, there is one's own ethical creed.

Nevertheless, I still have challenges. While I have worked in many categories from high technology to packaged goods, one area of expertise is marketing products to children. I even wrote a book on the subject entitled *Creating Ever-Cool.* There are those who objected to that part of my consulting business, saying that youth marketing, by its nature, is wrong. I must admit, I have thought long and hard about what I do, and the potential consequences. There are always issues that challenge character: How can we help millions of children smile, for example, without rotting their teeth in the process? How can we make millions of children laugh, without rotting their minds in the process? These issues are always with me as I struggle to ensure that the benefits of the products and services I help provide to children far outweigh the potential downside.

The social good of what each of us does and the specific good we do for our businesses is tested daily in individual meetings, individual moments, and individual decisions. When we have a set of principles and ideals we can refer to, it helps to set a tone and a direction.

Legend speaks of an ancient, authentic Code of Chivalry that all medieval Knights strived to achieve. It supposedly identified such virtues as bravery, self-denial, and generosity. Some historians say no such consistent, written code ever existed. Rather, a Knight's duties changed over time, and given the social circumstances, so did the ideals. Indeed, various Knights and others wrote about different virtues over time. But that matters little, for while the virtues may have shifted here and there, the basic intent stayed the same—to provide specific standards of behavior to help Knights and would-be Knights stay on a noble course. Only when those seeking knighthood achieved the necessary virtues would they kneel in gratitude to be *dubbed* a Knight. Importantly, knighthood could not be simply passed down in a family from one generation to the next. No one could be born a Knight. It had to be earned over many years of study and training. Even kings had to pass the test before they could receive the honor. That, perhaps most of all, is why the concept of knighthood has survived the ages, handed down in stories and songs. The *possibility* for knighthood is in all of us, at any level, if only we demonstrate the necessary character and competence that the honor demands.

The honor of knighthood can also be lost. In 1621, Sir Francis Mitchell was declared guilty of "grievous exactions." He was stripped of his knighthood at Westminster Hall. As part of the formal degradation, his belt was cut, his spurs smashed, and his sword was broken over his head. He was deemed "No longer a Knight but Knave."

I cannot help but think of recent high profile white-collar criminals who have been led away in handcuffs by police.

Knighthood *meant* something in those ancient days. It was an honor to those who were Knights themselves. It was an important goal to those who wished to achieve the honor. Moreover, it was the flesh and blood embodiment of noble standards.

In its own small way, that is the intent of *A Knight's Code of Business*. These are ancient precepts, reinvented for today's business professionals, that provide standards we must all strive to attain as we make our way within an organization, from Serf to Monarch. Much like the *practice* of medicine, we may never reach perfection, but our skills will sharpen with each new challenge successfully met, and we will learn with each misadventure absorbed.

The challenge is to continually strive for a purpose more noble than we had hoped and to act in an ethical and competent manner *even though no one may be looking*. We will fail at times. The objective, however, is to achieve high moral character and competence as often as we can, and to recognize those situations in which we begin to slip. That will make ourselves, and the institutions in which we work, magnificent.

On the following page, the reader will find *A Knight's Code of Business*, summarized from the pages of this book. Success for a Knight means achieving success for your company in a way that also holds true to character and competence. Again, that may sound silly in today's cynical world, but it is nevertheless true.

I encourage you to become a Knight in spirit. Slay the many dragons that attempt to make you and your kingdom weak. Rip *A Knight's Code of Business* out of this book, and nail it mightily upon your castle doors, so that all those who enter will know what is expected of them. It is a common language that all Knights can use, in all kingdoms, so that no matter where you travel, all will be aware of the ideals for which you strive. Moreover, when you meet another Good Knight, you will know him or her instantly, and woe to the Evil Barons that seek to subvert your kingdoms.

A Knight's Code of Business

Wisdom: A Good Knight strives for great wisdom, routinely promoting high moral character over low moral character, competence over incompetence, company interests over intense self-interests. Only then can all in the kingdom flourish.

Meritocracy: A Good Knight creates and defends meritocracies in the workplace, because such a system recognizes those who achieve, and compensates them accordingly.

Truthfulness: A Good Knight is honest, keeps promises, and does not get involved with duplicity of any kind, grand or subtle.

Law Biding: A Good Knight abides by laws of man and morality.

Decency: A Good Knight strives for decency in the workplace.

Bravery: A Good Knight must have a brave heart and work to eradicate fear throughout the entire kingdom.

Well-Being for Others: A Good Knight looks after the personal well-being of those entrusted to him, as well as those who are not, for the kingdom will be better for it.

Sincerity: A Good Knight will be sincere with all people, in ways that are direct though respectful, balancing the appropriate degree of praise and criticism.

Passion: A Good Knight is passionate about the craft.

Vision: A Good Knight protects and cultivates the visionaries, for they are the future of the realm.

Communication: A Good Knight listens carefully and communicates carefully to all those within the realm and beyond, in an honest and concise way.

Sustained Superiority: A Good Knight seeks sustained superiority through excellence, which can only come through sustained effort and periodic reinvention.

Sensibility: A Good Knight can distinguish tomfoolery from what truly matters, valuing substance above style, and placing humility before boastfulness.

Effectual: A Good Knight forces the kingdom to address the real problems, no matter how difficult the task, for that is the only way to slay futility.

Listing the code is one thing; living by it is quite another. I have known many that would espouse virtues in public, and then dispense poison in private. However, I have also had the good fortune to know a handful of men and women that I would consider to be truly Good Knights, people who have fought to achieve character and competence in the workplace, in public, and in private. One such Knight is Gary Elliott (though he is embarrassed by my giving him that title).

I first met Gary in the early 1980s when I joined Ogilvy & Mather in Los Angeles. He was in the account group and I was in the research department. He made an immediate impression upon me. His standards were high and often uncompromising, and they made mine higher. In time, Gary was not just an associate, but he became my boss as his authority and influence grew. Throughout, Gary's standards stayed high, an inspiration to all of us who worked with him. Today, Gary is a VP for Global Brand and Marketing Communications at Hewlett-Packard. Though we have not worked together for many years, to this day I still measure my performance by the criteria Gary set so long ago. While he provided a couple of stories for this book, and even commented on a draft, I asked Gary to grant me one last favor, to send me his thoughts on what it is like to be a Knight in today's world. Here's what he had to say.

On Being a Knight in Today's Business World
by Gary Elliott

A couple of things knighthood is not:
- *It is not easy.*
- *It is not often rewarded.*
- *And, most of the time, it is not wanted.*

Being a Knight is frustratingly hard.

It requires patience, maturity (a healthy balance of purpose and self), common sense, consistency, and resolve.

It calls on those passionate few that struggle so that talent wins out over politics, so that truth can triumph over innuendo.

It calls on those with a keen sense of calibration; for they know moral compasses get out of synch quickly in the business world.

It asks sacrifice from those who nurture and provide safe harbor for others needing guidance and support. And it demands strength and stamina to deal with distortion, stealth, and subterfuge.

Few people start out in business intentionally hurting others, stealing or lying. In other words, Evil Barons are rarely born.

Business is about producing results; attaining goals set by you or for you. Achieving those goals is where behavior is influenced, adapted and rewarded. The greater the reward—money, position, obligation, peer pressure, power—the greater the force bearing down on you. Many find their values change, slowly at first, until the castings become more unrecognizable.

It is hard to stay focused in business on what is truly important. Mahatma Gandhi said: "When I despair, I remember that all through history the way of truth and love has always won. There have been tyrants and murderers and for a time they seem invincible, but in the end, they always fall—think of it, ALWAYS."

Love and Truth always win out in the end.

So, why attack windmills? Why fight the fight? Why go against the odds?

I believe it is because we have to. The fight, in business or in your own personal life, is about each of us discovering who we are and identifying the metrics by which we can try to understand ourselves.

Lincoln offered up wise counsel on his own system of measurement. "When I do good, I feel good. When I do bad, I feel bad." I like that.

Being a Knight in the business world is about truly embracing life; and being a catalyst for others.

In the end, your word and your deeds define you. They precede you and follow you; they become your shadow and your light.

Do well.

With those words, I'll continue this chapter of *A Knight's Code of Business* by paying tribute to another great Knight who had the character, but unlike Gary Elliott, not the competence to match it. Alonso Quixano was a middle-aged gentleman struck with madness. In a world thick with vices, where power meant far more than honor, his mind chose a path of virtue that could only be achieved by accepting delusions and rejecting harsh realities. So Alonso donned his great grandfather's armor, mounted a skinny horse, recruited a loyal squire named Sancho, chose the chaste love of a woman he named Dulcinea, and renamed himself Don Quixote. He was reborn, with his mind retreating into an idealistic world of knights and honor and principles.

However, the world around him was absent of honor and cared little for principles, so he was rejected, ridiculed, and made sport of.

Cervantes used the sympathetic Don Quixote so convincingly that you root for this incompetent knight to succeed, to reestablish a piece of honor somewhere, somehow, thus to mark the place where a knight-errant once had been. You cannot help but realize that Cervantes, himself a maimed war hero, a prisoner of war, often poor, was a firm believer in chivalry, longing to attain ideals in a world that often refused to value them.

I could have made many parallels between Don Quixote's adventures and those of business professionals today. It could be said, for example, that Don Quixote's battle with the windmill represents our battles to fight bureaucracies and aristocracies. Or that his desire to attain the golden helmet of Mambrino represents our desire to obtain treasures that, like the helmet, are merely bronze when compared with riches that are more virtuous. Or that Sancho's quest to govern an island represents our desire for authority, filled with more farce than fact. However, those comparisons would have been forced. Rather, I let each chapter simply begin with a phrase uttered by Don Quixote in hopes that we could hear the purity of Cervantes' spirit whispering to us from across the ages.

The whispers said much. Cervantes told the tale of one honorable man who wanted desperately, passionately, to make a difference. It didn't matter that this man often stood alone. It only mattered that he stood. It didn't matter that he never reached his ideals. It only mattered that he tried. It didn't matter that no one shared his noble virtues. It only mattered that he held them dear. It didn't matter that he was ridiculed for his principles. It mattered only that he knew where truth lived. That is the legacy Cervantes left us. With a touch of Don Quixote's madness, we can achieve the same.

Don Quixote Epitaph

> *"Here lies the noble fearless knight,*
> *Whose valor rose to such a height;*
> *When Death at last did strike him down,*
> *His was the victory and renown.*
> *He reck'd the world of little prize*
> *And was a bugbear in men's eyes;*
> *But had the fortune in his age*
> *To live a fool and die a sage."*

—CERVANTES

Chapter 16

Leaving the Aristocracy

"You must know, friend Sancho, that the life of a knight-errant is subject to a thousand perils and mischances, yet equally they may possibly become kings and emperors, as experience has shown of various knights with whose histories I am thoroughly acquainted."

—Don Quixote

The corporate world is a nice place to work. Though grand misadventures make the six o'clock news and become topics of books such as this, they are the exceptions and not the rule. We spend most of our days within solid castle walls, doing what we do, in competent and ethical ways, with co-workers who do the same. Every now and then, an aristocrat may make an appearance, or someone will act in a duplicitous fashion, putting self-interests above company interests. In general, however, these tend to add more excitement than danger to our worlds. Even entrenched aristocracies can be made comfortable, as long as one knows the quirks of the nobles, the games they play, and how to negotiate one's way around the most treacherous of beasts—the Evil Baron. With your salary in hand and a lower or middle management position, you will be able to buy a nice home, raise a family, send your kids off to college, and save for a comfortable retirement. Yes, life inside the corporate world can be quite good. You might even make it into the highest reaches of the realm, and gain a coveted seat at the roundtable, where you can do great deeds.

Those who find themselves in environments that are more futile will have a far tougher life, indeed. However, the power is still theirs, either to change the institution in which they find themselves miserable, or to leave for other realms. That choice is always there. Yet I am always surprised at the number of people who will complain about their workplace, and yet neither change it nor leave it. They wallow in purgatory (we are all guilty of this at times).

The book *What Color is Your Parachute* notes that each year about "45 percent of all U.S. workers would change their careers if they could," but that only "10 percent of all U.S. workers actually do." That leaves 35 percent who want to change their careers, but do not. That is troubling.

Whether you find yourself in a comfortable corporate position, a boring one, or a hideous one, you can always use change. So leave. Go somewhere else. Start over. Jump career paths. That is a frightening concept, I know. However, many of us do not realize that, somehow, everything will work out okay anyway. We have been trained to believe that we must always ascend upwards through the ranks of an established institution. First, you get hired at entry level, and then you become a junior manager, then a middle manager, then a senior manager, then president, and finally CEO. Right? It's about upward movement. It's about linear progression.

But it doesn't have to be. If you discover that you do not have the ability, opportunity, or inclination to make it to the very top of some established kingdom, and haven't a parachute large enough to carry you away to early retirement, you might consider another course. Instead of climbing to the very top, fall instead to the very bottom. It can be a very nice place to land.

I should explain.

FALL TO THE BOTTOM

When I started my career at General Mills, I was a newly minted MBA with a strong desire to pull myself up one step at a time. I had aristocracy on my mind, and a desire to become a Monarch, if only in the department. Yet I was near the bottom of my career path. This was hard to swallow, because when you got an MBA in 1980, you mistakenly thought you were at the top. Business magazines told us so.

Anyway, what gave me a bit of satisfaction was realizing that, despite the fact that I was near the lowest rung of my career path, I still had a virtual army at my command. These armies were my vendors. They were truly at the bottom, I reasoned, because they reported to me. There were independent research companies, consultants, moderators, and even independent illustrators who would draw itsy-bitsy pictures of new product concepts that I would send into testing.

I even felt a bit guilty at times, as some of my *minions* were much older than I, which made me feel saddened that they should have to report to me, a virtual infant in the business world. However, I wouldn't feel too sad for long, for I was the gifted MBA, and they were not. The world had order to it, and I was going places. It also didn't matter that they always seemed happier than I. That only meant that I was busier. That somehow made me more important, too.

Then I noticed something odd. At the end of one particular day as a meeting with one of my independent illustrators came to a close, we walked to the parking lot together. I jumped into my 10-year-old Pontiac with well over 100,000 miles on it, and my independent illustrator jumped into his new Porsche, waving and smiling as he passed me on the road.

"Must have been an inheritance from a dead aunt," I thought. "That would also explain why he's so happy all the time." Besides, he could not possibly afford that car on what I paid him. I did a little math, assuming that he had 10 clients who gave him the same amount of business as I did, and came up with a salary for my independent illustrator. My estimate staggered me. "No," I thought, "It can't be that high!" I tucked the incident in the back of my mind, and didn't give it another thought. I was the boss, he was at the bottom, and life was good that way. I had the soul of an Aristocrat on the salary of a Page.

Fast-forward about 10 years to 1991. I was now the senior partner at Ogilvy & Mather Advertising, with a seat on the executive committee, and a flattering reputation in many parts of the kingdom (at least that's what I like to think). Life was good. Then one day after attending some focus groups, I walked to the parking lot with the independent moderator that my people had hired for that evening. I jumped into my five-year-old Honda Accord, whereas he jumped into his

$40,000 Mercedes (in 1991), while explaining that he keeps the really expensive Mercedes—his other car—at home. He wasn't kidding. "No," I thought, "Can't be." This guy is at the bottom of the food chain, not at the top. I hired him. I'm the chief, the guy in charge, and the leader. He smiled and waved as he left me.

"Where have I seen that smile before?" thought I.

Then it struck me. What the independent illustrator and the independent moderator had in common was simple: they were INDEPENDENT. They were no longer part of the Aristocracy, no longer subject to the political intrigue, and no longer confined to pay scales dictated by the nobles. "That's it!" I said. These are the artisans and craftsmen that every company needs to make their castles a beautiful place in which to work.

At the same time, I was beginning to lose interest in the hierarchy, the promotions, the rank, and the perks. This became clear one afternoon when my boss turned to me and said that he wanted to begin grooming me to run an office in a city of my own. While flattered, I suddenly realized I didn't want that. It didn't seem as important any more. I longed for something else that I could not get within the castle walls. I wanted a sense of freedom, to control my own destiny, and to spend more time with my family. I even authored a "My Turn" article that appeared in the September 23, 1991 issue of *Newsweek*. The title of the article was *A Question of Loyalty* and I used the forum to discuss the rapid decline of company loyalty (deservedly so). Maybe I had just grown tired of the castle, but I suddenly realized that a hierarchy does not have to be scaled, nor do you need to be concerned with who is on top and who is on the bottom. Hierarchies suddenly seemed to take themselves too seriously.

To achieve independence, I suddenly realized that I needed a craft, a specialty beyond the more general nature of my day-to-day functions. I needed to be recognized for something specific. Then my boss, Jerry McGee, stuck it in my face. He told me to gather all the knowledge I had accumulated over the years in one particular category where I had extensive experience, youth marketing, and write a book. I did, and entitled it *Creating Ever-Cool, A Marketers' Guide to a Kid's Heart*. I launched it into the world and it was a success. Not because the book made a lot of money (it didn't) but because it positioned me as a specialized craftsman.

So I took a deep breath, and stepped outside of Ogilvy. I was snapped up instantly in a deluge of projects. I have worked with all levels, from chairmen to presidents to VPs to freshly minted MBA's. I love spanning organizations from top to bottom, and get excited by the insights that come from all. I have become a reflection of the moderators and illustrators and consultants I knew so many years ago, when I was too young to realize that by going to the bottom, they were already at the top. And while youth marketing helped to position me as a craftsman to get a foot in the door, clients soon discovered the other business skills I had developed over the years, and began to employ those skills as well in a host of consulting endeavors.

Though I started my own company, I refuse to make it an aristocracy. I built a home office and now only hire others on a temporary basis when projects demand. If I were to rent an outside office, I figured, I would need to hire a receptionist or secretary, and that alone might cause an aristocracy to form. I refuse to take part in that.

I have also developed a much healthier sense of my business worth. During one of my first meetings as an independent consultant, I was ushered into the offices of one of the largest entertainment companies in the world, before one of its presidents. During this introductory meeting, I provided not only my credentials, but a 20-minute presentation on what I thought were the key challenges he was facing, my initial hypotheses that articulated ways to address the challenges, and then a research plan as to how we could, together, discover the truth. Near the end of the meeting, my blood froze when he asked me where my "offices" were. I suddenly felt very small, but there is nothing like the truth, so I told him I worked out of my home, and left it at that. I was told after the meeting that I was actually pitching against an international consulting company with offices around the world. I left the meeting, suddenly deflated. In the presence of a king, I suddenly looked like a homespun simpleton working out of his garage.

The next day, I was awarded the project. This president cared about craftsmen, and for some reason, found what he needed in me. I will be forever grateful for that moment, because it said that I had value as a craftsman, even though I had stripped myself of the corner office, the title, and the accoutrements that accompanied my life in the aristocracy I left behind. I am still learning from those nobler than I am.

From the outside looking in at so many companies, things became clearer. I'd say that as an independent craftsman, 90 percent of my job is spent on the craft—the work. When I was inside the company, I would say that 30 percent really had to do with the work. The rest was about maintaining the company itself—the people, hiring, firing, raises, politics and so on. That's why I think companies need craftsmen, because they realize we are able to focus efforts in ways that the organization cannot, and to develop in-depth skills in ways that organizations cannot.

I work more hours now, but I see my family more because I work at home. Clients only call if they really need me, and only call back if they appreciated the work. I can sometimes see the politics that exists in companies, but I am shielded from it. I make enough to keep my home, get my kids through college, and save for retirement. And I smile more. Independence does that.

This was all because I took the time to position myself via a book, took the risk, and had the good fortune to find a collection of great clients who value what I do. I practice competence and character on a daily basis as best I know how, and I have had luck in finding clients that practice the same.

The point of all of this: it's not about the company you work for, or where you stand in the hierarchy, or your salary, or the perks, or the size of your office, or your title. It's about you. It's always about you. It is about who you are inside, and the way that manifests itself in your character and your competence. Be consistent in what you do. Be excellent in what you do. Then no matter where you travel, whether you are a Knight within a kingdom, or a Knight for hire, or a craftsman who peddles his wares from realm to realm, you will be of worth to those in the marketplace and, more importantly, to those at home.

I hope my book will provide an insight or two. I also hope it isn't *too* preachy. Thank you for taking the time to read it. Farewell and Godspeed.

Gene Del Vecchio
Squire-in-Training

Appendix

Kingdom Characters Quiz

Do you walk on the EVIL side? Do your fellow employees? Take the test!

Below are 10 incomplete sentences that describe how people might react to various situations, along with four possible endings for each situation. Circle the ending that best describes how you would most likely react.

1. **When you first read stories about Enron and WorldCom, you . . .**
   A: Were saddened that evil was running rampant, and began to look even closer at your own company's practices.
   B: Were concerned at the thought that your own company might be at risk, but you did not know what to do about it.
   C: Felt envious that there's a lot of loot out there, but you don't have any of it.
   D: Berated your finance department for not showing that kind of initiative, and then instructed them on finding even more devious plots that the government would not detect.

2. **You've seen a lot of press about company stock options, and thought . . .**
   A: I'm glad people are discovering just how damaging they can be.
   B: Options . . . what are options?
   C: Options . . . why don't I have any options?
   D: Let me see . . . I have 100,000 options . . . I need to convert them before some goodie-goodie tries to take them away.

3. **Your Human Resources department hired a consultant to instruct employees about sexual harassment, so you . . .**

   A: Rounded up all your employees to make sure they understand the issues.

   B: Are glad to attend because you know it's important and you need to learn.

   C: Want to go because the topic makes you *hot*.

   D: Made it a personal goal to have sex with the instructor.

4. **You have an opportunity to get a well-deserved raise, but it means you have to lay off a good employee to do it, so you . . .**

   A: Pass on the raise and save the person.

   B: Go to someone you trust for advice because you are struggling slightly with the decision.

   C: Take the raise and sleep well that night.

   D: Take the raise, then cheat the laid off employee out of the severance pay he had coming, convincing yourself that he didn't deserve it anyway.

5. **Your primary goal is to . . .**

   A: Make your company the best it can be.

   B: Learn all you can because you want desperately to contribute more.

   C: Get ahead while covering your mistakes, for you covet titles more than brain cells.

   D: Crush anyone in your company who tries to thwart your rise to the very top.

6. **You're truly innovative when it comes to . . .**

   A: Motivating people to do great work.

   B: Listening intently and learning new skills.

   C: Getting others to do your work.

   D: Finessing your company's financial records.

7. The last time you screwed up, you immediately . . .

A: Took responsibility, fixed the problem, and then moved on.

B: Panicked, but eventually took the blame, and then tried to fix it as best you could.

C: Accused others, everywhere, in all directions, throughout the known universe.

D: Had a scapegoat already identified, then fired the guy and announced "all is now well."

8. Fellow associates who are in need of help find that . . .

A: You are the first person they can go to for advice and resources.

B: You might not have the answers, but you'll break a limb to get them.

C: They should best leave you alone, because you're too busy for them.

D: It's easier to get a juicy bone out of a dog's mouth, than to get helpful information or resources from you, for you know that such things constitute power.

9. You are asked to give a big presentation next Tuesday, and you immediately . . .

A: Begin to identify substantive matters important to the audience.

B: Realize it's a great opportunity to show what you know, though you are worried you'll screw up.

C: Try to pawn it off on someone else.

D: Think about how you can influence your audience with charisma, style, and bravado.

10. You hear that an Evil Baron works upstairs, so you . . .

A: Come to alert, lance in hand, ready to defend your company and fellow executives.

B: Hide, knowing you are no match.

C: Seek him out, hoping to learn much under his or her tutelage.

D: Come to alert, lance in hand, ready to defend your turf from someone more unscrupulous than you.

Now, add up the number of times you circled A, B, C, or D, and place them here:

A _____

B _____

C _____

D _____

If most of your answers are "A", chances are you are a Good Knight, with high moral character and high competence.

If most of your answers are "B", chances are you are a Good Squire-in-Training, with high moral character and increasing (though underdeveloped) competence.

If most of your answers are "C", chances are you are an Evil Henchman, with low moral character and low competence.

If most of your answers are "D", one might expect you to be an Evil Baron, with low moral character yet high competence. However, true Evil Barons are too shrewd to be caught with this game; they more likely answered "A" all along, knowing that great power can be had if they appear to be Good Knights. Those who answered "D" are more likely to be Henchmen with delusions of grandeur.

Note: While this quiz may appear to be frivolous, the truth is that as you survey your own company, you are apt to find many traits mentioned in this quiz throughout your organization. These classifications are all too real.

Index

⁓

About the Author

GENE DEL VECCHIO is an independent consultant. His assignments are quite broad, though he specializes in brand strategy, advertising, and research.

Gene offers a unique perspective on the business world in general, having worked on the client side, the agency side, as researcher, as strategist, as employee, and as part of management. Over his 20+ year career, he has also worked across many business categories and with some of the most prominent companies in America and even the world, including Disney, General Mills, IBM, Kraft Foods, Mattel, Microsoft, Nestle, Pacific Bell, PacificCare, Paramount Pictures, and many more.

Gene began his career at General Mills as a researcher where he helped launch new products and rejuvenate old ones. Soon afterwards, he left for Ogilvy & Mather, one of the world's most venerable advertising agencies. Gene stayed 17 years, becoming a senior vice president (later named senior partner). Importantly, he held a seat on the Executive Committee in which he shared responsibility for office stewardship, profits and losses, hiring and firing. Though Gene's functional duties included planning & research, at various times he was asked to lead training, human resources, and even company morale as part of his management role.

Gene has two books to his credit. His latest is *A Knight's Code of Business*, which serves to help managers achieve high moral character and competence in today's corporate world. His first book was *Creating Ever-Cool*, which helped marketers develop brands that kids would love and parents would appreciate.

Gene is a guest speaker at various conferences, and has expressed his many views in the press. He has received several advertising industry Effies, a David Ogilvy award, and WPP's prestigious Atticus Award, all given for his contributions toward effective brand strategy. Gene holds an MBA from USC and a BA, Phi Beta Kappa, from UCLA.

Among the bad news: 26 percent agreed that their company is sometimes run like an *aristocracy*, in which authority is concentrated in a few top executives who sometimes seem to get more rewards than their fair share.

A Knight's Code of Business is not a dry read, but a fun and insightful one, filled with real stories and advice that can help any executive become a Knight in his or her business realm.

A Knight's Code of Business is a call for executives to join the *knighthood* and foil the attempts of those *Evil Barons* among us who serve to satisfy their intense self-interests to the detriment of their companies and their fellow employees.

GENE DEL VECCHIO is an independent consultant. He offers a unique perspective on the business world, having worked on the client side, the agency side, as researcher, as strategist, as employee, and as part of management at Ogilvy & Mather in Los Angeles where he shared responsibility for profit and loss, human resources, company morale, training, and more. Over his 20+ year career, he has also worked across many business categories and with some of the most prominent companies in America and even the world, including Disney, General Mills, IBM, Kraft Foods, Mattel, Microsoft, Nestle, Pacific Bell, PacificCare, and Paramount Pictures. Gene received his BA in economics from UCLA, and an MBA from USC.